BOOK I

DECODING THE LAWS OF THE UNIVERSE

METAPHYSICAL INTERPRETATION

O.M. KELLY

COPYRIGHT

Copyright © 2023 Margret Ann Kelly/O.M. Kelly
Series: Book I (Revised)
First Published as Book I in "Decoding the Mind of God",
Margret Ann Kelly/O.M. Kelly, Copyright © 2011.
ISBN: 978-0-6452492-3-1

All rights reserved. This book may not be reproduced, wholly or in part, or transmitted in any form whatsoever without written permission from the author, O.M. Kelly, www.elanea.com.

The author of this book does not dispense medical advice or prescribe the use of any technique as a form of treatment for physical, emotional, or medical problems without the advice of a physician, either directly or indirectly. The intent of the author is only to offer information of a general nature to help you in your quest for emotional and spiritual well-being. In the event you use any of the information in this book for yourself, which is your constitutional right, the author assumes no responsibility for your actions.

AUTHOR

Author O. M. Kelly, known as Omni to her clients and students is an accomplished author and international lecturer, on Metaphysics, Philosophy and understanding the Collective Consciousness. Omni consults for Member States of the European Commission as a Conciliation Advisor and Rhetoric Counsellor for other International Companies throughout Europe. Omni now resides on Australia's beautiful Gold Coast, writing books, and works as a Life Mentor and Business Coach.

Omni has dedicated her life to decoding the mysteries of the universe. With a deep knowledge of the biblical agenda, mythologies including ancient Egyptology, Asian principles, and metaphysical insights, Omni has discovered the secret that all stories share a coded hidden metaphysical language. Her seminal work, "Decoding the Mind of God", is a compilation of nine volumes of metaphysical information based on the research into the coded information of the Laws of the Universe, also known as the Collective Consciousness, and represents a groundbreaking contribution to our understanding of the metaphysical universe. Now, all nine volumes are being released as separate, revised books, each offering a unique perspective on the universe's workings. Omni's work has been widely acclaimed for its depth of insight, and her contributions to the field of metaphysics have been groundbreaking.

THIS BOOK

If you're looking to unlock the hidden potential within you and transform your life, "Decoding the Laws of the Universe" is the book for you. This powerful and insightful book is designed to help you understand the deeper, metaphysical aspects of life and tap into the transformative power of the universe utilising the secrets of our Individual Universal Law.

This book serves to introduce you into the secrets of our Individual Universal Law. This amazing knowledge and wisdom, is transformative on a personal level and creates the opportunity for you to interrelate with the Laws of the Universe. Throughout this book, you will dive deep into the inner workings of your mind and discover the hidden laws that govern your life. You will learn about the alchemy of the mind and how to harness its power to create positive change in your life and the world around you. Through the lens of Metaphysical philosophy, you will gain a new perspective on the world and your place in it. You will learn how the universe communicates with you through coded intelligence and how to unlock the hidden messages that are all around you.

This book is a journey for personal transformation and spiritual growth. Take a voyage of exploration of the expansive vistas of information discovering the codes of Metaphysics and the Quest of Life. You will learn the Metaphysical coded wisdom of the ancients for the necessary mind elements to transit into a higher mindset. Explore the secret relationship between the Earth and human beings, the higher mind, the Metaphysical journey, the importance of self, belief in self, the codes of mythology, a higher level of attainment, releasing the past, fears and evolving one's light on a Metaphysical level, what causes stress, work place promotion and why it does not happen, and many other topics. Included is a short overview of the conventional Twelve Laws of the Universe.

CONTENT

Introduction

Chapter One
Our Individual Universal Law And The Laws
Of The Universe — Page 1

Chapter Two
The Twelve Laws Of The Universe—An Overview — Page 14

Chapter Three
A Secret Relationship Between The Earth And
Human Beings — Page 38

Chapter Four
When We Take The Metaphysical Journey — Page 41

Chapter Five
The Hierarchical Mind — Page 46

Chapter Six
When You Learn To Become The Trunk Of Your
Own Tree Of Knowledge — Page 50

Chapter Seven
The Importance Of Self And The Evolution Of
Consciousness — Page 53

Chapter Eight
Releasing The Past, Fears, And Evolving One's
Light — Page 57

Chapter Nine
The Wheel Of Life — Page 68

Chapter Ten
Mythology Is A Coded Intelligence — Page 70

Chapter Eleven
Metaphysical Interpretation Of Myths — Page 73

Chapter Twelve
Our Futuristic Time Locks — Page 82

Chapter Thirteen
My Journey — Page 84

Chapter Fourteen
A Higher Level Of Attainment And What Is
Your Heart's Desire?   Page 88

Chapter Fifteen
Stress Levels—Becoming The Boundary Rider   Page 95

Chapter Sixteen
Understanding The Value Of You   Page 98

Chapter Seventeen
The Master Gardener—Chen   Page 102

Chapter Eighteen
Personalities—Aspects of Self   Page 105

Chapter Nineteen
The Laws Of The Universe And Promotion In
The Workplace   Page 110

Chapter Twenty
When We Ask The Universe For An Answer   Page 116

Chapter Twenty One
The Inner Kaleidoscope   Page 121

Chapter Twenty Two
Opening The Heart   Page 127

Chapter Twenty Three
Masters Of Time   Page 130

Chapter Twenty Four
Time Is Not At All What It Seems   Page 135

Chapter Twenty Five
The Final Chapter   Page 138

Appendix A   Glossary   Page 143

Books by O.M. Kelly (Omni)   Page 150

INTRODUCTION

You are the most important person on this Earth.
Omni

The wisdom you have learned on your life's journey up to this point is perfect for you; I am not here to take anything away from you. I am explaining the next step on your life's quest, and my hope is that my story will give added value to your own strength, assisting you to understand yourself, your own Individual Universal Law and how we exist within a greater Universe that has its own proprietary law as well. You will ascend into a higher knowing of how you can live out your own intelligence. This journey you are beginning to unravel is an unfolding of your inner wisdom, and that wisdom is the formation of your truth.
Omni

CHAPTER ONE

Our Individual Universal Law And The Laws Of The Universe

Introducing our Individual Universal Law and the Laws of the Universe.

It is our own Individual Universal Law creating the Laws of the Universe! It is where we all become involved, and, through time and cause and effect, we have created and advanced our evolution for all humanity to inherit. The Laws of the Universe, (also known as the Universal Law, the God essence and other terminology), is the Soul Energy of the Collective Consciousness; it is a mathematical program of all that is.

It is the Soul's purpose (each person) to be here on the planet, and each Soul must release and improve the energy that has collected from the past. We are asked to live and discover this inner truth that is embedded in the depths of the Laws of the Universe, which are embedded in each one of your cells. We have evolved for a very special reason.

Our own Individual Universal Law refers to the Metaphysical philosophy that each individual is responsible for creating their own reality through their thoughts and emotional intelligence. The nature of each person's thinking, unique perspective and energy contributes to the overall consciousness of the universe. This knowledge is transformative on a personal level; once we understand, we can make great waves for all of humanity to inherit.

OVERVIEW:

<u>Our Individual Universal Law</u>

We are each our own Universe with our own Individual Universal Law, and we exist within a greater Universe that has its own proprietary law as well.

You are your own Universal Law; and, as you think, so, too,

you create. You are given this gift to be in charge of how your thoughts create your world. As you allow one thought to finish itself, the next one is waiting to release itself to you. Your next thought will wait patiently until you are silent enough to allow it to come through.

Your Individual Universal Law is not created by what you do, but, rather, by your silent thoughts, regressions (thinking in the past), joys, frustrations, and peace. It is the energy and evolution of your emotional intelligence and how you connect to you.

Once you understand what your Individual Universal Law is, keep yourself focused, and you will be able to fulfil all your desires. Life will bring you up, through the temperance of your Soul, and, when you can define this inner education, you will become the Divine.

The Laws of the Universe

It is our Individual Universal Law creating the Laws of the Universe! It is where we all become involved, and, through time and cause and effect, we have created and advanced our evolution for all humanity to inherit. These Laws of the Universe are also known as the following: Collective Consciousness, Universal Law, the God essence, Collective Library of the Consciousness, World Consciousness, Collective Inheritance, Collective Memory, Collective Mind, Collective Soul of the God Force, Akashic Hall of Records, Hall of Recognition, Soul Energy of Collective Consciousness, and other terminology.

The Laws of the Universe (Collective Consciousness) registers all our conscious thinking, which must return to the conscious mind in order for our energy to continue to grow through the human evolution. The past is still alive in the Collective Consciousness; that Collective Inheritance is all of our thinking and evolution. We cannot forget yesterday, but we can absorb it; we can soak it up into our own consciousness and use it in the moment.

The Laws of the Universe answers to our thinking in a balanced way, but it is not always in the way that we expect it to be!

Another name for it is Karma, or the "Kha-Rha-Mha", if we explain it correctly, for this goes back to the early language of the Armenians and the hieroglyphs of Egypt. If we pronounce it in its correctness, it is the cause and effect, or the accidental and occidental; it is the occidental that is the key to your wisdom. The occidental is the final outcome of the length of your stay on this planet. The occidental is the light that keeps this planet alive.

So, your knowledge of these secrets can carry you to the place where you have the opportunity to dance along with these Laws of the Universe.

As you begin to believe in yourself, your Soul (your Soul is your life force) gives you never-ending gifts of knowledge. To believe in yourself takes a tremendous amount of courage, and that courage will lead you into other parallel worlds of existence. Those worlds align within and open you up to your inner worlds, and then you have earned the freedom to use them to promote your tomorrows.

EXPLAINED FURTHER—DELVING DEEPER:

Our Individual Universal Law

Let us explore further, our own Individual Universal Law. As stated previously your Individual Universal Law is not created by what you do, but, rather, by your silent thoughts, regressions (thinking in the past), joys, frustrations, and peace. It is the energy and evolution of your emotional intelligence and how you connect to you.

Understanding and connecting with our emotional intelligence is key to tapping into our Individual Universal Law. This involves becoming aware of our thoughts, of our emotions, learning to identify and process them, and understanding the ways in which they influence our actions, and outcomes we experience in life. By paying attention to the patterns and themes that emerge in our lives, we can begin to identify the underlying beliefs and values that shape our perceptions of reality.

Our emotional intelligence is instrumental to the evolution of our Individual Universal Law. Our emotions are energy in motion, and they have a vibrational frequency that attracts experiences and circumstances of a similar frequency. When we are in a positive emotional state, we are vibrating at a higher frequency, and we tend to attract positive experiences and people into our lives. Conversely, when we are in a negative emotional state, we are vibrating at a lower frequency, and we tend to attract negative experiences and people into our lives.

Therefore, to evolve our Individual Universal Law and attract more positive experiences into our lives, it is crucial to work on our emotional intelligence and maintain a positive emotional state as much as possible. This means being aware of our emotions, expressing them in healthy ways, and choosing to focus on positive emotions such as love, gratitude, joy, and a feeling of peace with oneself. We can use mindfulness, staying in the moment and have an awareness of the chatter of the mind.

We can also examine your "relationship of self". Your relationship of self is the way you relate to you. It is created by the thoughts you have about yourself, belief in self, the emotions you feel in regards to yourself, your judgements about yourself, your perception your self-worthiness and how you honour yourself—and the big one, your internal dialogue to self. When your belief in self builds upon its own strength and creates your next positive thought, your life becomes so much easier for you to manage.

How can we improve our relationship with ourselves, and what steps can we take to cultivate a more positive internal dialogue that supports our self-belief and self-worth? How can we break free from negative thought patterns and judgments about ourselves, and build a stronger foundation of self-love and self-acceptance that empowers us to create a more fulfilling life? How can we identify and change limiting beliefs that may be holding us back, and replace them with more empowering beliefs that support our growth and development? The answer is by cultivating a positive internal dialogue. Improving our relationship with ourselves involves several steps. Firstly, we need to become aware of our current internal dialogue and how we talk to ourselves. We can start by observing our thoughts and emotions, and noticing any patterns of negativity or self-judgment. Once we have identified these patterns, we can work on changing them by replacing negative self-talk with positive self-talk and affirmations of "I believe in myself". To cultivate a more positive internal dialogue, we can furthermore practice self-compassion and self-forgiveness. To break free from limiting beliefs and judgments about ourselves, we can challenge these beliefs and reframe them in a more positive and empowering light. This can involve seeking out new perspectives and information, and exploring new ways of thinking and being. When your belief in self builds upon its own strength and creates your next positive thought, watch how the miracles manifest in your life where you will find you are continuously working as one with the universe.

This journey is yours and cannot be given to anyone else; the responsibility is yours alone. The hierarchical mind/unconscious mind/higher mind, also known as the Higher Self, will always be there to step in front of you, protecting and holding you firmly when you cannot believe or when you have lost your trust in you. Our Higher Self is a deeper and evolved aspect of our being and has access to higher levels of wisdom, intuition, and guidance. Our Higher Self, presents experiences for us. It gives us the opportunity for our thoughts to repeat throughout our life until we can find the strength to overcome them. This suggests that our Higher Self may be trying to teach us something or help us grow by presenting recurring negative thoughts, experiences, or fears.

Our thinking can create our fear in the moment by the way we perceive and interpret our experiences. Our thoughts and beliefs about a situation can trigger a fear response in our body, even if there is no actual physical threat. Our thoughts can also create a negative feedback loop, where the fear response reinforces the negative thinking, leading to more fear and anxiety. By changing our thinking and challenging our beliefs, we can break this cycle and reduce our fear and anxiety in the moment. If you find yourself repeatedly experiencing negative thoughts, fears, or experiences, it is important to stop them before they become greater. Remember the traffic lessons you learned in school: **stop, look,** and **listen**. Take a moment to search beyond the present moment and see how this energy or thought is recreating itself. To search beyond the present moment, is to take a step back and analyze the situation objectively. One way to do this is to observe the thoughts and feelings that arise when the negative thought, experience or fear resurfaces. Ask yourself questions such as: What triggered this thought or feeling? What emotions am I experiencing? Is there a pattern to these thoughts and feelings? Reflect on how this thought or fear has impacted your life and try to gain insight into why it keeps coming back. This process of self-reflection can help you identify the underlying causes of the negative thought or fear and find ways to overcome it. This is not a learning experience, but an earning experience. The difference between the two is that learning means "looking at" something, while earning means "looking through" it. Your Higher Self, presents these experiences to you as an opportunity to overcome them. One thing in life is certain: You cannot run away from yourself. There is nowhere to hide!

You create your fear in the moment through your thinking. Write this down: "My fear is created by me, as I am refusing to live and accept this Divine moment in my life." By acknowledging your power over your thoughts, you can take the first step towards personal transformation.

If I can help you to understand and accept, where you can act out your thoughts through self-confidence and assurance; and then we are both winners. Hopefully you will have the opportunity to rake away your fears, as this is the sole—and Soul—reason for you to be here, and it is what this life's quest is all about. We rake up all the leaves after the autumn season has ended, and we prepare the garden for winter. Winter is the time for hibernation, and it is through our own hibernation that we are given the time to dichotomize, which means to sort out right from wrong and refrain from making the same mistakes. When we look out our window again, our garden looks tidy and free; the raking has allowed it to regain its own silence and to breathe new life as it prepares to birth itself for the next season.

For years in the journey to discover this metaphysical knowledge (that is, before I became an Adept in the Secrets), I went into the "Worlds of Invisible Kingdoms" (explored other dimensions) and was asked by my teachers to read the Bible in the reverse from Revelations back to Genesis, instead of the other way around. It is not necessary for you to do this. My teachers informed me that, by doing this, I could bring through a resonance of intelligence that all of humanity could view from within themselves—where they could understand the capabilities of how their intelligence unfolds itself, and then that knowledge would be available for them to add to what they had already achieved. "Why?" I asked my teachers. "Your program fits the bill" they told me. "What program?" I persisted. "The thoughts of your previous generations have been indelibly imprinted in you, and you have made yourself available; you asked, so now you have the opportunity to receive!" That's what they told me!

To further explain, a "life program". Your life program was created through your parents' DNA, which provided the basic principles for you to become you. Your task is to unfold yourself through the disadvantages of your parents' judgment and (mis)understanding themselves! You have chosen to live what your parents were too afraid to face through their acceptance of self as they understood it, and, more importantly, you have also chosen to live their gains.

Your life program keeps on creating itself through each of your thoughts building upon the other, and the transformation continues until you have taken your last breath. That energy force field grows in strength and opens you up into your Higher—or heavenly—Self. That Higher Self follows you through every thought you think, always encouraging you to create and expand your thinking.

To carry your DNA inheritance into your next step of humanity's earnings is how and why you have evolved to be here, through balancing and clearing your past generations' thinking and programming the basics of the mind of your future generations. Once you have accepted this program, it is no longer a detriment to your consciousness; the freedom you create in your mind will allow your intelligence to have the ability to evolve even further. Once we have recognized and solved the tasks that have been given to us by our genetic inheritance, we are free to collect more information to add to the benefits available to us beyond this program.

During those years of my internal searching, my intelligence grew into the "Wisdom of the Sages", where I could see through the layers of restriction that I had hidden behind for my own protection. I also began to study the science behind humanity's thinking, and, as this information grew, understanding it fully became my ultimate goal; as a result, over the years, all knowledge consumed me. I found I could unite the plumber with the librarian, the lawyer with the builder, the electrician with the social worker, and then unite them all into a whole! It is the relationship of self that connects us to the energy of our total evolution.

This knowledge has grown stronger and stronger over the last thirty years of my life. Subsequently, I brought all this information into a format that is ongoing in every moment of my life. I learned how to transfer this knowledge into the human body by beginning with just one cell.

Once you understand what your Individual Universal Law is, keep yourself focused, and you will be able to fulfil all your desires. To keep ourselves focused and fulfil our desires according to our Individual Universal Law, we need to maintain a clear and positive mindset. This means consistently monitoring our thoughts and redirecting any negative or limiting beliefs towards positive and empowering ones. We can do this by practicing mindfulness and being present in the moment, observing our thoughts and choosing to let go of any that do not serve us. Visualization and affirmations can also be powerful tools to help us stay focused and aligned with our desired outcomes. By visualizing ourselves already having achieved our goals and repeating positive affirmations that affirm our abilities and worthiness to receive what we desire, we can tap into the power of our Higher Self and attract more of what we want into our lives.

Life will bring you up, through the temperance of your Soul, and, when you can define this inner education, you will become the Divine.

The Laws of the Universe

Let us explore further The Laws of the Universe. As stated, it is our Individual Universal Law creating the Laws of the Universe! It is where we all become involved, and, through time and cause and effect, we have created and advanced our evolution for all humanity to inherit. The Laws of the Universe (Collective Consciousness) registers all our conscious thinking, which must return to the conscious mind in order for our energy to continue to grow through the human evolution. The past is still alive in the Collective Consciousness; that Collective Inheritance is all of our thinking and evolution. We cannot forget yesterday, but we can absorb it; we can soak it up into our own consciousness and use it in the moment.

The Collective Consciousness registers all our conscious thinking by storing and recording every thought, emotion, and experience in a universal database or energy field. It is the energy of the thought, emotion, and experience that registers with the Collective Consciousness on a quantum level. Basically explained on a quantum level, our thought energy interacts with the universe through the observer effect. This effect describes how the act of observation can change the behaviour of particles and systems in the universe. When we focus our thoughts on something, we are essentially observing it with our consciousness, and this observation can affect the behaviour of particles and systems related to that thing. According to quantum physics, all particles and systems in the universe are interconnected and entangled. This means that our thoughts and intentions can have an impact on the behaviour of these interconnected particles and systems. Our thoughts and emotions emit energy waves that can influence the energy of the Laws of the Universe, the Collective Consciousness. (The physical particle-like structure of matter existing in time-space, in which it exists non-locally "encoded" as a wave frequency in the past, present and future of the Collective Consciousness—the holographic universe).

This collective inheritance of knowledge and wisdom is available to us all and can be tapped into for personal growth and evolution. (Time-space reality is the frequency domain of the Higher Mind as well as the Collective Consciousness). As individuals contribute their thoughts and experiences to the collective, the database expands and evolves, contributing to the evolution of humanity as a whole.

As previously mentioned, The Laws of the Universe answers to our thinking in a balanced way, but it is not always in the way that we expect it to be! Another name for it is Karma, or the "Kha-Rha-Mha", if we explain it correctly, for this goes back to the early language of the Armenians and the hieroglyphs of Egypt. If we pronounce it in its correctness, it is the cause and effect, or the accidental and occidental. It is the occidental that is the key to your wisdom. The occidental is the final outcome of the length of your stay on this planet. The occidental is the light that keeps this planet alive. That gift from the All That Is, is our attainment, and it is also how we have produced our next moment. Weather patterns, diseases, viruses, and wars are all creations of the atmospheric conditions of the Collective Consciousness; they are the results of the thinking of this planet. Our accidents are what we have produced for ourselves through our thinking. The occidental is the explanation, as to how we have gathered and achieved the accident in the first place. It is not only what you have done to you; it is how the Laws of the Universe answer back to what you are doing to you. I like to refer to the occidental as the "messenger" represented as the Pigeon throughout the Laws of Shamanism. With its sonic sound, it homes in on a catastrophic conclusion of thought, and then it delivers the message to our heavenly home, which is our brain.

A Brief Metaphysical Overview Of The Brain/Mind

A brief description of the structure of our brain/mind (a metaphysical interpretation): Our brain has two sides. The left brain is our logic (conscious mind). The left brain is our masculine side; our ego, our primal fear, and as stated our logic. It represents how we are representing ourselves to others through releasing from within. The right brain is our emotions (subconscious mind). The right brain is our feminine side, our inner creativity. We give out to others with the right side, and our energy in motion—or emotion—creates itself from how we are giving and receiving to and from the self. The right brain represents what we are doing to ourselves within, and what we are capable of receiving through ourselves–through our being aware of that giving.

The people who live in their logical ego sense are perfect, and so, too, are the people who live in their creative emotional sense. In understanding the logical sense, we understand through our primal inheritance, where it begins to fit with common sense. The mind of logic is the echo from whatever is created, and it is also what we attract in our outer worlds; the emotional mind sits within and takes care of our sense of responsibility.

We cannot survive on this planet without both ego and emotions. Our journey is to learn how to balance both brains so that we may become aware of the supportiveness of our unconscious mind/higher mind. The unconscious/higher mind, also known as our Soul/Higher Self, is the freedom with which we can tune into understanding ourselves, but only when the other two have balanced through our attitude to our self. We touch and connect to our unconscious mind/higher mind, as the other two brains encompass the Soul through looking into one another.

If we like to take this further; our left brain, our conscious self, is responsible for the first and second-dimensional mind. Our right brain, our subconscious self; is responsible for the third dimension and the relationship to the introduction of the fourth dimension. The balance of both brains is the doorway up into our unconscious mind/higher mind, which allows it to be responsible for the temple of self to live up to its expectations. Through balancing your mind, you uplift your emotions, and you become not only more aware of your intelligence but also more emotionally aware. This emotional intelligence is a reasoning of perpetual motion, which continuously balances and harmonizes your mind, body, and Soul, and which also equates to your family, friends, and country. The whole planet has the opportunity of continually harmonizing and reflecting itself back to you, and this reflection is the mind, body, and Soul of all.

Temple of self relates to the training of our self, moment by moment, where we learn to have a deeper understanding as to how we balance and control our thinking. It is where we earn the right to be in control of the incessant chattering that the ego likes to try to regain and re-control every situation as it did before! Our unconscious/higher mind is the make-up of our Divine Inheritance—or the language of our Soul—it is our life force. The unconscious mind/higher mind is the world of telepathic communication that every person tunes into on an etheric level, whether they believe in it or not. It is the ultimate reason you are here experiencing your life's journey.

***

I wrote my books for you, not your friends or family. The purpose of my work is to explain, in written form, the quest of your own intelligence, where you will realize that you have no limits as to discovering your outer boundaries. I would like you to learn how to understand yourself first. Only through understanding yourself do you have the opportunity to nourish and nurture others. Allow your family and friends the opportunity to make their own mistakes, and they will then learn to earn their own gains. Through understanding this message, you are conforming through a state of Grace. On my journey I discovered in my reading research it was the little things such as in Galatians 5:1: "Stand fast therefore in the liberty wherewith Christ hath made us free, and be not entangled again with the yoke of bondage." Which means, do not become entangled with your fear to the point where your own restrictions bind you. I discovered thousands of verses like this, and they helped me release the pressures of my past's hold on me—at last, through my awareness, I could see how my past tried to control me, but I also saw how to watch it surrender as it grew steadfast within itself!

Another little verse that gave me sustenance throughout the journey was from the Book of Thomas in verse 2—which is one of my favourites, as it reveals many answers—this verse is about the words spoken by Jesus: "Let him who seeks continue seeking until he finds. When he finds, he will become troubled, he will be astonished through his own revelations, and he will rule over the all." This passage explains the search for self. Once we have suffered enough through not being able to understand ourselves our fear immediately jumps to attention—simply because it has no other direction to take. We become troubled when we cannot see or hear our next step. These words were a great revelation to me as I fumbled and stumbled along.

Read on, and the Universe will return to you all the answers that you need to unfold your truth.

Your Notes:

CHAPTER TWO

The Twelve Laws Of The Universe— An Overview

Although this book serves to introduce you into the metaphysical secrets of our Individual Universal Law, I have included an overview of the conventional referenced Twelve Laws of the Universe. An overview of the most popular is as follows:

The Law Of Divine Oneness: Everything and everyone is connected and part of a larger whole.

The Law of Vibration: Everything in the universe vibrates at a certain frequency.

The Law of Correspondence: As above, so below. The patterns and characteristics in the universe also exist within us.

The Law of Attraction: Like attracts like. Our thoughts and emotions attract similar experiences into our lives.

The Law of Action: To manifest our desires, we need to take action towards them.

The Law of Cause and Effect: Every action has a consequence or effect, whether positive or negative.

The Law of Compensation: The universe always seeks balance, and our actions and thoughts determine what we receive in return.

The Law of Perpetual Transmutation of Energy: Energy is constantly flowing and changing form.

The Law of Relativity: Everything in the universe is relative and only has meaning in relation to other things.

The Law of Polarity: Everything has two poles, positive and negative, and both are necessary for balance.

The Law of Rhythm: Everything in the universe has a rhythm or cycle of ups and downs, and we can learn to navigate them.

The Law of Gender: Everything in the universe has masculine and feminine energies that work together for creation and manifestation.

<u>The Law Of Divine Oneness</u>: Everything and everyone is connected and part of a larger whole.

The Law of Divine Oneness is a fundamental principle of metaphysical philosophy, which states that everything in the universe is interconnected and part of a larger whole. This law entails there is a universal consciousness (Collective Consciousness) that permeates everything and everyone, and that we are all part of this divine energy.

This law presents that the separation we experience in our physical reality is an illusion, and that we are all part of a unified field of consciousness. Everything we do, say, or think affects this field of energy, and in turn, it affects us (as it is within, so, too, it is out there; every other human on this planet is representing to you a part of yourself. We are all one).

This law is often associated with the concept of non-duality, which is the belief that there is no separation between the self and the universe. Non-duality suggests that we are not separate from the universe, but rather we are a part of it. We are all one, and what we do to others, in reflection, is also a mirror image of what we are also doing to ourselves.

Metaphysical example:

In Ancient Egyptian mythology, the Law of Divine Oneness was an important principle that governed the workings of the universe. The ancient Egyptians believed that everything and everyone was connected and part of a larger whole, and that this interconnectedness was essential to the functioning of the universe. According to ancient Egyptian mythology, the god Atum was the creator of the universe and the source of all life. Atum was believed to have created the world out of his own body, and everything in the universe was seen as an extension of Atum's divine essence. The ancient Egyptians also believed in the concept of Ma'at, which was the principle of harmony, balance, and order in the universe. Ma'at was embodied in the goddess of the same name, and was seen as the foundation of all life and creation. The Law of Divine Oneness was closely tied to the concept of Ma'at, as it emphasized the interconnectedness of all things and the importance of maintaining balance and harmony in the universe. The ancient Egyptians believed that all things were part of a larger whole, and that every action had a ripple effect that could impact the entire universe. The Law of Divine Oneness also emphasized the importance of recognizing and honouring the divine essence in all things, including other people, animals, and the natural world. By acknowledging the interconnectedness of all things and treating everything with respect and reverence, the ancient Egyptians believed that they could maintain balance and harmony in the universe.

<u>The Law Of Vibration</u>: Everything in the universe vibrates at a certain frequency.

The Law of Vibration is a metaphysical principle that everything in the universe vibrates at a certain frequency. This means that everything, from the smallest subatomic particle to the largest galaxy, is in a constant state of vibration or motion.

Every object, thought, and emotion has a specific vibration or frequency. These vibrations can be measured using tools such as frequency meters or oscilloscopes. Every living being, including humans, also has a unique vibrational frequency. Your Soul's journey is through the vibrational energy that releases from your thoughts—whether that be positive or negative energy. This law is closely related to the concept of energy. All matter is made up of energy, and energy is what gives everything its unique vibrational frequency.

This law has important implications for our lives. Our thoughts, emotions, and actions influence the frequency at which we vibrate. Positive thoughts and emotions vibrate at a higher frequency, while negative thoughts and emotions vibrate at a lower frequency. Therefore, if we want to attract positive experiences into our lives, we need to focus on positive thoughts and emotions and raise our vibration. We are all connected through this energy, as to how we can influence others by raising our own vibration. When we vibrate at a high frequency, we can positively affect those around us and create a ripple effect of positive energy. Overall, the Law of Vibration reminds us that everything in the universe is connected through energy.

Metaphysical examples:

Excerpt from the book by O.M. Kelly "Book II. Decoding Thought", Chapter excerpt from, The Power of Thought:

When turkeys use force to empower their wings to scrape along the ground, the sound is like that of a drum; they are sending out a vibration to attract the lower, or earthly, kingdoms to pay attention to their tone.

***

Excerpt from Chapter 10 of this book:

On the journey of life you have developed and expanded your aura, and that aura is collected through the vibrations of your thoughts manifesting by means of the mathematics that the metaphysical system of the Laws of the Universe creates.

***

Excerpt from the book by O.M. Kelly "Book II. Decoding Thought", Chapter excerpt from, Your Law of Self:

When we receive a species of the plant kingdom internally, we also receive the vibration of the species' emotion. The emotion of the plant is the Alchemy of its life force; the mathematics is its creation, which has ensued continually throughout its evolution. It is also instilled in our understanding of our third-dimensional mind. Plants are a living energy here to serve us in the same Collective Consciousness. When we place that plant into our mouth, chewing and swallowing it, the essence from the food moves up into the brain through the two small holes in the roof of the mouth, and then that essence registers itself with the unconscious/higher mind, which allows the mathematics to register in the brain. This acts as a mirror of the species vibrating and accepting one another. The brain registers that it has received this energy, and it has the opportunity to use this mathematical frequency at any time to repair a difficult thought that we cannot bring into abeyance. It is a species of our intelligence. It is an accepted spark of our Universal Law.

<u>The Law Of Correspondence</u>: As above, so below. The patterns and characteristics in the universe also exist within us.

The Law of Correspondence is a metaphysical principle that acknowledges the patterns and characteristics of the universe which also exist within us. This law highlights that the universe is a reflection of ourselves, and that the macrocosm (the larger universe) and the microcosm (the individual) are interconnected and share similarities.

The phrase "as above, so below" is often used to describe this law, and it explains that the patterns and dynamics that exist in the universe are also present within us. For example, the movement of the planets in our solar system can be seen as a reflection of the cycles of birth, growth, and change that occur within us.

The Law of Correspondence denotes that we can learn about ourselves by observing the patterns and cycles of the universe. By recognizing the similarities between the outer world and our inner world, we can gain a deeper understanding of ourselves and our place in the universe. For example The Laws of the Universe (Collective Consciousness) registers all our conscious thinking, which must return to the conscious mind in order for our energy to continue to foster and grow through the human evolution.

This law also suggests that we have the power to shape our reality through our thoughts and actions. By aligning our thoughts and actions with the patterns and characteristics of the universe, we can create positive change within ourselves and in the world around us.

Overall, the Law of Correspondence reminds us that we are interconnected with the universe and that the patterns and dynamics of the universe also exist within us. By recognizing this interconnectedness, we can gain insights into ourselves and our place in the world, and use this knowledge to create positive change in our lives which echo out to the world around us.

Metaphysical examples:

Excerpt from the book by O.M. Kelly "Decoding the Shaman Within":

Cairo was previously called "EL-Kha-He-Rha", which, when decoded means "through everlasting life our knowledge heavenly ascends through to the heavenly energy, and releases us up into heavenly ascension". Wow! Many mentions of heaven here; three, to be exact: one for each level of God. Remember that the word "through" means "seeing from within". What a title! This is a grand commission for the people of Cairo to live up to and call home. Cairo is also referred to as the "home of the Pyramids". If we care to look from the right side of the head into the matter of the brain, we see the three glands: hypothalamus, pineal, and pituitary. These three glands are placed inside the brain in identical unison to the way that the Pyramids are placed in Egypt. They do not align through the left side of the head. Remember that the <u>mind of the Universe is identical to the mind of the human body.</u>

To my understanding, the smallest Pyramid is the small gland of the hypothalamus; the middle one is the pineal, which is slightly above the other two; and the largest, the pituitary, relates to the Great Pyramid of Chi-Ops. This is the story of the mythical Pharaoh, known through the codes as the unconscious Energy (Chi or Che) of the Oracle, which is the Power of the Soul (OPS).

In the Great Pyramid of Cheops there are two shafts that

penetrate into what is known as the King's Chamber in a northerly and southerly direction. In the same analogy as the brain, through my estimation, I believe that, what is referred to as the King's Chamber is the home of the pineal gland. These two shafts are directing the energy flow into both the left and right hemisphere of the brain at the same time; as explained through the opening of the heart ceremony described in Egyptology, which occurs when the right brain has been freed by the restriction of the ego through releasing its hold or control over the mind. We also note that there are seven steps leading into the grand gallery, all of which reminds us of the seven vertebrae of our neck area, or the seven bands of peace through Egyptology, another reference is the seven seals, or the seven churches of Asia from the last book of the King James Bible, as to how we have exonerated ourselves. Now you are becoming aware of the myths and stories of Egypt, as well as the Bible, which are both explaining to us the Atlas of the human body, which are the road maps, as to how we connect on an inner level to ourself.

***

Excerpt from Chapter 14 of this book:

Mythology began to explain itself back through the twelve houses of the Gods or the Twelve Houses of the Astrological Signs. It is a mirror guiding us up towards the entrance into the unconscious/higher mind. This is where we enter up into the home of the High Priest, the Sage, the Shaman, and the Prophet. They represent personalities that have collected and earned their written stories, as a result of having entered up into these higher territories. We have entered into the realm of non-judgement; which becomes the realm of justice! It is the only way we can enter! Now can you understand the stories from the Egyptian hieroglyphs that are carved on the walls of the temples, regarding Astrology, the language coming from the stars? Once we have passed through the medulla oblongata, we have left our three-dimensional reality—we are living in the afterlife.

The Milky Way is symbolically representing the ideas that are available for us to release back into the Universe, all in the service of helping others.

***

In ancient Egyptian mythology, the Law of Correspondence (as now known by this name), was a fundamental principle that emphasized the interconnectedness of all things in the universe. According to this principle, the patterns and characteristics that exist in the universe also exist within us, and by understanding these patterns, we can gain insight into the nature of the universe itself.

The ancient Egyptians believed that everything in the universe was interconnected and that the macrocosm was reflected back into the microcosm. They believed that the gods, the stars, and the natural world all had corresponding aspects within the human body and psyche.

For example, the god Horus, who was associated with the sky and the sun, was also seen as a symbol of spiritual vision and insight within the human psyche. The goddess Isis, who was associated with the moon and the cycles of nature, was also seen as a symbol of fertility and the nurturing aspect of the feminine within human relationships.

The Law of Correspondence was closely tied to the concept of Ma'at, which was the principle of harmony, balance, and order in the universe. The ancient Egyptians believed that by understanding the correspondence between the macrocosm and the microcosm, they could align themselves with the principles of Ma'at and maintain balance and harmony in the universe. Overall, the Law of Correspondence was a fundamental principle in ancient Egyptian mythology that emphasized the interconnectedness of all things in the universe. By recognizing the patterns and characteristics that exist within us and in the world around us, the ancient Egyptians believed that they could gain insight into the nature of the universe and align themselves with the principles of harmony, balance, and order.

<u>The Law of Attraction</u>: Like attracts like. Our thoughts and emotions attract similar experiences into our lives.

The Law of Attraction is a metaphysical principle that acknowledges that like attracts like. Our thoughts and emotions have a powerful influence on the experiences that we attract into our lives.

This law reflects the understanding that the universe is made up of energy and that everything in the universe is connected. Our thoughts and emotions are also forms of energy, and they vibrate at a certain frequency.

For example, if we have positive thoughts and emotions, we attract positive experiences into our lives. On the other hand, if we have negative thoughts and emotions, we are more likely to attract negative experiences.

The Law of Attraction has been popularized in recent years with the use of vision boards and journaling in attracting what we would like in our life by intention. Many people find the Law of Attraction to be a useful tool for creating positive change in their lives. By focusing our thoughts and emotions on what we want to attract, we can create a more positive mindset and take actions that are in alignment with our desires. This can help us to achieve our goals.

Overall, allow me to reiterate, that the Law of Attraction acknowledges that our thoughts and emotions have a powerful influence on the experiences that we attract into our lives. By focusing on positive thoughts and emotions, we can create a more positive mindset and attract experiences that are in alignment with our desires.

Metaphysical examples:

Excerpt from the book by O.M. Kelly "Book IV. Decoding Death", Chapter excerpt from, Parallel Worlds:

I would like to make a short reference here to a learning I received through watching the Olympic Games. The journey began when some athletes won their medals. Each person's life story emerged during the final gathering of their previous ninety-day period – that is, before the Olympic Games. It all depended on the Law of Attraction as to how the athletes' minds had collected on behalf of themselves. It was through their genuine belief and knowing that they were good enough, through their deliberation, to attract their final outcome. They had earned these medals. The mathematics had already decided on the outcome. It made no difference which sporting field they were representing; they had earned the specified ignition through their own forthrightness.

***

Excerpt from the book by O.M. Kelly "Book VII. Decoding Sacred Fung Shwa", Chapter excerpt from, The Quest of Life:

The more respect we give to ourselves, the more our thoughts have the ability to strengthen. That is the Law of Attraction. Our illusion pulsates and creates the hidden strength of our own reflection. Through earning the stillness within the self, the vibration of trillions of your cells attracts attention to you. Stillness alerts the unconscious/higher mind. This is how we learn to accept the continuance to enter into the fourth dimension of reality.

***

Excerpt from the book by O.M. Kelly "Book IX. Decoding Extra-Terrestrial Intelligence", Chapter excerpt from, The Extra-Terrestrial is Your Next Realm of Self:

Thought attracts thought, energy attracts attention, and like attracts like. The Law of Attraction spins its web to help us connect to our intelligence; this is the gift that the Collective Consciousness returns to us, and we as individuals have the ability to share that same unconscious/higher mind with ourselves. It is a nice Palace or place to live in, when you become aware that there is nothing that you do not have an answer for!

***

A metaphysical interpretation: In ancient Egyptian mythology, in reference to the Law of Attraction (as we know the name now), the ancient Egyptians believed that their thoughts and emotions had the power to attract similar experiences into their lives. They believed that the gods and goddesses of the universe were constantly responding to the thoughts and emotions of humans. Metaphysically interpreted the god Thoth, who was associated with wisdom and knowledge, was often depicted with a pen and a writing tablet, symbolizing the power of the written word to manifest reality. The goddess Bastet, who was associated with pleasure, and joy (reference from Herodotus writings), was seen as a symbol of the power of positive emotions to attract positive experiences into their lives. (Bastet received many depictions.)

The ancient Egyptians also believed that negative thoughts and emotions could attract negative experiences into our lives. The god Set, who was associated with chaos and destruction, was seen as a symbol of the destructive power of negative thoughts and emotions.

<u>The Law of Action</u>: To manifest our desires, we need to take action towards them.

The Law of Action is a metaphysical principle that acknowledges that to manifest our desires, we need to take action towards them. This law is based on the fact that we are co-creators of our reality, and that we have the power to shape our lives through our thoughts, emotions, and actions.

The Law of Action emphasizes the importance of taking deliberate and intentional action towards our goals and desires. This action can take many forms, such as setting specific goals, creating a plan of action, and taking steps towards achieving those goals.

While positive thinking and visualization are important, they are not enough on their own. In order to manifest our desires, we need to take steps towards them. This means taking action even when we may not feel motivated or inspired, and persisting in the face of obstacles and setbacks.

The Law of Action also emphasizes the importance of taking responsibility for our own lives and experiences. This means recognizing that we have the power to shape our lives through our actions, and that we cannot rely on external factors or other people to create the life we want.

Overall, the Law of Action reminds us that we have the power to shape our lives through our thoughts, emotions, and actions. By taking intentional action towards our goals and desires, we can manifest the life we want and create positive change in the world around us.

Metaphysical Example:

Excerpt from the book by O.M. Kelly "Book II. Decoding Thought", Chapter excerpt from, The Alchemy of the Brain:

The Lady of the Lake, of course, is the emotional mind keeping the sword (the "Soul's word") in her command. She lives in the waters—that is, the Collective Consciousness. Remember that the word is mightier than the sword. The rest of the story is in relationship to the personalities (aspects of self) that Arthur had to birth in order to bring himself together to become his temple mind. Every story is exactly the same; they had to wander through the experiences of their past to achieve and accomplish their freedom.

We can only remember the myth or truth of yesterday when we quickly override our negative thinking. It cannot store itself, and yet the truth can. It is a pronounced energy that is automatically held through the Collective Inheritance. That is just one of the wonderful stories of how every human can understand him/herself. Metaphysically, the sword is the cross we accept—it is our mind. The cross is the light, as well as the shadow self. In other words, when we need our own protection we hold our fear close to the heart. This is number four in the Sacred Numerology, which is the temple of self. We are <u>training our self</u>, moment by moment, to have control over our thinking, which explains why the sword is always placed in the right hand. It is showing us that this is our <u>inner action</u>; which can only be achieved once we have opened our heart to release the Divine Intelligence through our selves.

<u>The Law of Cause and Effect</u>: Every action has a consequence or effect, whether positive or negative.

The Law of Cause and Effect is a metaphysical principal that acknowledges that every action has a consequence or effect, whether positive or negative. This law is based on the belief that the universe operates according to a system of cause and effect, and that every action we take has an impact on the world around us. Every thought, word, and action we take has a corresponding effect on our lives and the world around us. This effect can be positive, negative, depending on the nature of our actions and intentions. We must be mindful of the impact our actions have on ourselves and others, and strive to act in ways that are aligned with our values and intentions.

Overall, the Law of Cause and Effect reminds us that every action we take has a corresponding effect on our lives and the world around us. By acting with intention and mindfulness, we can create positive effects in our lives and contribute to the well-being of others as well as the world around us.

Metaphysical Examples:

Excerpt from Chapter 1 of this book.

The Laws of the Universe answers to our thinking in a balanced way, but it is not always in the way that we expect it to be! Another name for it is Karma, or the "Kha-Rha-Mha", if we explain it correctly, for this goes back to the early language of the Armenians and the hieroglyphs of Egypt. If we pronounce it in its correctness, it is the cause and effect, or the accidental and occidental; it is the occidental that is the key to your wisdom. The occidental is the final outcome of the length of your stay on this planet. The occidental is the light that keeps this planet alive.

Accident: Our accidents are what we have produced for ourselves through our thinking. Our thinking produces energy. For example, anger can build up in negative energy and if not released through reasoning an accident will occur.

Occidental: The occidental is the explanation, as to how we have gathered and achieved the accident in the first place. The occident is how we created that accident through our mathematics being realigned to our thinking. The occident is another way to explain the Laws of the Universe in action. The mathematical codes have clicked into action and been brought together!

***

In ancient Egyptian mythology, the Law of Cause and Effect was closely tied to the concept of Ma'at, which was the principle of harmony, balance, and order in the universe. The ancient Egyptians believed that every action had a consequence or effect, and that these consequences could be positive or negative depending on the nature of the action.

The goddess Ma'at was often depicted holding a set of scales, symbolizing the importance of balance and justice in the universe. The ancient Egyptians believed that if a person's actions were in alignment with the principles of Ma'at, they would be rewarded with positive consequences, such as prosperity and good health. On the other hand, if a person's actions were in opposition to Ma'at, they would face negative consequences, such as illness, poverty, or even death.

The ancient Egyptians also believed in the concept of karma, which stated that our actions in this life would have consequences in future lives. They believed that the afterlife was a continuation of the earthly life, and that the consequences of our actions would be felt in both realms.

<u>The Law of Compensation</u>: The universe always seeks balance, and our actions and thoughts determine what we receive in return.

The Law of Compensation is a metaphysical principle that acknowledges that the universe always seeks balance, and that our actions and thoughts determine what we receive in return. This law is based on the belief that everything in the universe is interconnected, and that every action we take has a corresponding effect on the world around us.

According to the Law of Compensation, the universe seeks to restore balance and harmony whenever there is a disruption.

This means that if we engage in positive actions and thoughts, we are likely to receive positive outcomes and rewards. On the other hand, if we engage in negative actions and thoughts, we are likely to experience negative consequences and setbacks.

The Law of Compensation acknowledges that we are responsible for our own lives and experiences, and that we have the power to shape our reality through our actions and thoughts. This means that we must be mindful of the energy we put out into the world, and strive to act in ways that are aligned with our values and intentions.

Metaphysical example:

In ancient Egyptian mythology, the Law of Compensation (as known by the name now) was closely related to the concept of Ma'at, which was the principle of harmony, balance, and order in the universe. The ancient Egyptians believed that the universe was always seeking balance and that our actions and thoughts determined what we would receive in return.

The Law of Compensation was a fundamental principle in ancient Egyptian mythology that emphasized the importance of our actions and thoughts. By aligning ourselves with the principles of Ma'at and taking responsibility for our actions, the ancient Egyptians believed that they could maintain harmony, balance, and order in the universe and ensure a positive outcome for themselves and future generations.

<u>The Law of Perpetual Transmutation of Energy</u>: Energy is constantly flowing and changing form.

The Law of Perpetual Transmutation of Energy is a metaphysical principle that acknowledges energy is constantly flowing and changing form. This law is based on the understanding that everything in the universe is made up of energy, and that this energy is constantly in motion and undergoing transformation.

According to the Law of Perpetual Transmutation of Energy, we have the power to shape the energy in our lives through our thoughts, emotions, and actions. This means that we can influence the energy around us and transform it into something that is more positive and beneficial.

For example, if we focus our thoughts and emotions on positivity, gratitude, and abundance, we attract more of these energies into our lives. Similarly, if we take actions that are aligned with these energies, we are likely to experience more positive outcomes and opportunities.

On the other hand, if we focus our thoughts and emotions on negativity, fear, and scarcity, we are likely to attract more of these energies into our lives. Similarly, if we take actions that are aligned with these energies, we are likely to experience more negative outcomes and challenges.

The Law of Perpetual Transmutation of Energy reminds us that we have the power to shape our reality through our thoughts, emotions, and actions. By consciously directing our energy towards positivity and abundance, we can create a more fulfilling and joyful life for ourselves and contribute to the well-being of others and the world around us.

Overall, the Law of Perpetual Transmutation of Energy emphasizes the importance of being mindful of the energy we are putting out into the world and using this energy to create positive change and transformation in our lives and the lives of others.

Metaphysical examples:

Excerpt from the book by O.M. Kelly "Book VI. Decoding The Dolphin's Breath", Chapter excerpt from, The Story of Dolphins:

Dolphins: The mother of the baby dolphin is there as a support system and source of nurturing. This continues until the baby dolphin can allow its feelings—or security—to link with the movement, sound, pulse, and tone of the ocean; and to acknowledge the ocean to work with its thinking, which allows it to become at one with the ocean and all the oceanic species. This occurs through the hologram that is automatically created through the dolphin's mind becoming harmonized and mirroring back to itself. It releases a tone of mathematics— or codes—that enables it to create a life of perpetual ascension. Its continual state of mind becomes a focused movement which then carries it forward. That is why the dolphin's mouth is open all the way through to its crown. The same explanation relates to the whale and other similar species as well.

***

Excerpt from Chapter 1 of this book.

Through balancing your mind, you uplift your emotions, and you become not only more aware of your intelligence but also more emotionally aware. This emotional intelligence is a reasoning of perpetual motion, which continuously balances and harmonizes your mind, body, and Soul, and which also equates to your family, friends, and country. The whole planet has the opportunity of continually harmonizing and reflecting itself back to you, and this reflection is the mind, body, and Soul of all.

***

In ancient Egyptian mythology, the concept of the Law of Perpetual Transmutation of Energy was closely related to the belief in the cyclical nature of life and the universe. The ancient Egyptians believed that everything in the universe was constantly in motion, and that energy was constantly flowing and changing form.

The Law of Perpetual Transmutation of Energy emphasized the importance of this constant flow and transformation of energy in the universe. The ancient Egyptians believed that by aligning themselves with the natural cycles of energy and focusing their intentions, they could manifest their desires and achieve their goals.

The Law of Relativity: Everything in the universe is relative and only has meaning in relation to other things.

The Law of Relativity is a metaphysical principle that suggests that everything in the universe is relative and only has meaning in relation to other things. This means that nothing exists in isolation and that everything is interconnected and interdependent.

According to the Law of Relativity, the meaning of any experience or situation is relative to our own perspective and the context in which it occurs. This law reminds us that our perception of reality is subjective and that our experiences are shaped by our thoughts, beliefs, and emotions. What may be perceived as a challenge or a setback by one person may be perceived as an opportunity or a learning experience by another.

The Law of Relativity also emphasizes the importance of seeing the interconnectedness of all things and recognizing that everything in the universe is part of a larger whole. This means that every action we take and every thought we have has an impact on the world around us and the people in it.

By recognizing the relativity of everything in the universe, we can cultivate a sense of empathy and understanding towards others, as well as a greater appreciation for the diversity and complexity of the world we live in.

Overall, the Law of Relativity reminds us to see the world through a lens of interconnectedness and to be mindful of how our thoughts, beliefs, and actions impact ourselves and others. By recognizing the relativity of all things, we can cultivate a greater sense of compassion, understanding, and interconnectedness in our lives and in the world around us.

Metaphysical Example:

In ancient Egyptian mythology, the concept of relativity can be seen in the way they understood the world around them. For example, the Nile River was a vital part of their lives and was seen as a source of life and fertility. However, its importance and meaning only existed in relation to the desert that surrounded it. Without the harsh and barren landscape, the Nile would not have been revered and celebrated in the same way.

Similarly, the gods and goddesses of ancient Egypt were often depicted in relation to one another. Ra, the sun god, was seen as the most powerful deity, but his power was relative to the other gods and goddesses who played their own unique roles in the Egyptian belief system.

The Law of Relativity reminds us that everything in the universe is connected and only has meaning in relation to other things. We cannot fully understand or appreciate something without considering its relationship to everything else. In ancient Egypt, this concept was reflected in their understanding of the world and the interplay of the natural and supernatural forces that shaped their lives.

<u>The Law of Polarity: Everything has two poles, positive and negative, and both are necessary for balance.</u>

The Law of Polarity is a metaphysical principle that acknowledges that everything in the universe has two poles, positive and negative, and that both are necessary for balance. This law is based on the concept of duality, which suggests that everything in the universe has its opposite.

According to the Law of Polarity, positive and negative are not opposing forces, but rather complementary aspects of a single whole. For example, light and dark are not separate forces, but rather different aspects of the same phenomenon. The Law of Polarity also emphasizes the importance of balance and recognizing the value of both positive and negative aspects of life. Without darkness, we cannot appreciate the light.

Overall, the Law of Polarity reminds us to recognize the duality of life and the importance of balance.

Metaphysical examples:

Excerpt from the book by O.M. Kelly "Book VII. Decoding the Sacred Alphabet and Numerology", Chapter excerpt from, Ages of the Collective Soul:

We are aware, through the strength of the myth, that we have twelve strands to our DNA; metaphorically, this refers to the twelve Apostles, Disciplines, or Disciples that help us weave our web. We have twelve strands that are delivered unto us from above, and these twelve relate to the right hemisphere of the brain. We also have another twelve strands that reach up from our primordial past, which is known as our ego; the ego works in concordance with our left brain, and these other twelve strands relate to it. These twenty-four strands, together, create the double helix of our complete DNA, and both sets of twelve strands must learn to live in a habitual resonance with one another. There are twelve from the <u>light worlds</u>, and twelve from the <u>darkness</u> of our past. The past belongs to the Netherworld; the light worlds are our availability to create our future intelligence to support us along the way.

***

Excerpt from the book by O.M. Kelly "Book VII. Decoding the Sacred Alphabet and Numerology", Chapter excerpt from, The White and Blue Nile:

In the Sudan area, is situated the Sun Temple with its four statues relating to Ramses II. The number four (4) in Sacred Numerology decodes as the temple, which is the home of our dark and light worlds. Those four statues are symbolically referring to the balance of both brains that we must achieve to continue up into the afterlife!

***

Excerpt from the book by O.M. Kelly "Book IX. Decoding Extra-Terrestrial Intelligence", Chapter excerpt from, Releasing the Divinity Within You:

You create what you think, and, as you think, your energy goes out into the Collective Consciousness, where it forms its own life force. That life force must go somewhere; if you do not take responsibility for yourself, it must be reflected to the next person who thinks just like you do.

Remember that the dark and light forces are equal—it is not a war between the two—it is the acceptance of each that releases our free will, which promotes our freedom to express ourselves.

***

In ancient Egyptian mythology, the concept of polarity can be seen in the way they understood the natural world. They recognized that everything had two opposite yet complementary forces that worked together for balance and harmony. For example, the sun and the moon were seen as opposing forces that together created the cycle of day and night, and the flood and drought of the Nile River were seen as two necessary phases for the land's fertility.

The Law of Polarity reminds us that everything in the universe has two opposing forces that work together for balance and harmony. It teaches us that we cannot fully appreciate the positive without experiencing the negative and that both are necessary for growth and transformation. In ancient Egypt, the concept of polarity was fundamental to their understanding of the world, and it was reflected in their art, mythology, and religious practices.

<u>The Law of Rhythm</u>: Everything in the universe has a rhythm or cycle of ups and downs, and we can learn to navigate them.

The Law of Rhythm is a metaphysical principle that everything in the universe has a rhythm or cycle of ups and downs. This law is based on the idea that everything in the universe moves in cycles, from the seasons of the year to the cycles of the moon and the tides of the ocean.

According to the Law of Rhythm, everything in the universe moves in cycles of expansion and contraction, growth and decay, birth and death. This rhythm is a natural part of life, and we can learn to navigate it by recognizing and embracing the cycles of life.

The Law of Rhythm reminds us that change is a natural and inevitable part of life. We cannot always control the events that occur in our lives, but we can learn to adapt and navigate them by recognizing the rhythms and cycles that are already at work.

This law also emphasizes the importance of balance and resilience. When we recognize that life moves in cycles, we can learn to ride the waves of change and maintain a sense of balance and equanimity through the ups and downs of life.

Ultimately, the Law of Rhythm reminds us to be mindful of the rhythms and cycles of life, and to embrace the natural ebb and flow of the universe. By recognizing the natural cycles of life and learning to navigate them with grace and resilience, we can cultivate a greater sense of peace, balance, and harmony in our lives which autonomically vibrates to the world around us.

Metaphysical examples:

Excerpt from Chapter 17 of this book:

Turning Point: Through our allotted time, a self-awakening (review) automatically happens twice a year. In March through to April—it is known as the "Ides of March". One must turn around and face up to the responsibility of oneself! Again it occurs in mid-August through to September, when it is known as the "Winds of Change". Through the Laws of Shamanism, we refer to both of these stages as the "Turning Point". Every human has the opportunity to turn and face themselves (metaphorically); once after our summer months, and once after the winter, to review our life and face up to the responsibilities of self that we have forced ourselves to overlook. (By the way, through the interpretation of the Greek and Roman myths, the "Ides of March" was known as a day of infamy all through the assassination of Julius Caesar).

***

In ancient Egyptian mythology, the concept of the Law of Rhythm was closely related to the belief in the cyclical nature of the universe. The ancient Egyptians believed that everything in the universe, including the stars, the seasons, and the cycles of birth and death, followed a natural rhythm or pattern.

The ancient Egyptians also believed that the cycles of life and death were interconnected, and that the process of death and rebirth was a necessary part of the cycle of life. This belief was reflected in their funerary practices, which focused on preparing the body for the journey to the afterlife and ensuring that the deceased had everything they needed to navigate this transition.

Overall, the Law of Rhythm was a fundamental principle in ancient Egyptian mythology that emphasized the importance of recognizing and embracing the natural cycles of life and the universe. By learning to navigate these cycles, the ancient Egyptians believed that they could achieve greater harmony and balance in their lives and ultimately reach a higher level of spiritual awareness.

The Law of Gender: Everything in the universe has masculine and feminine energies that work together for creation and manifestation.

The Law of Gender is a metaphysical principle that acknowledges that everything in the universe has masculine and feminine energies that work together for creation and manifestation. This law is based on the concept of polarity, which suggests that everything in the universe has its opposite and that these opposites work together for balance and harmony.

According to the Law of Gender, masculine and feminine energies are not necessarily gender-based, but rather qualities or energies that are present in all things. Masculine energy is associated with qualities such as action, logic, and analytical thinking, while feminine energy is associated with qualities such as intuition, emotion, and creativity.

These energies are not opposing forces, but rather complementary aspects of a single whole. The Law of Gender reminds us that both masculine and feminine energies are necessary for creation and manifestation in all areas of life, from personal relationships to professional endeavours.

In essence, the Law of Gender suggests that everything in the universe has a masculine and feminine aspect, and that these energies work together to create balance and harmony. When we can recognize and balance these energies within ourselves and in our relationships, we can manifest our desires more easily and achieve a greater sense of harmony and balance in our lives.

Overall, the Law of Gender reminds us to embrace the complementary energies of both masculine and feminine, and to work towards balance and harmony in all aspects of our lives. By recognizing and balancing these energies, we can manifest our desires more easily and cultivate a greater sense of peace and harmony in our lives and in the world around us.

Metaphysical example:

Akhenaton, a beautiful being of light, represented the purification of his intelligence that he was both male and female. This explains his body shape that is recorded in his statues. He was announcing to us the next evolutionary step that humanity can step up into, which is the Metaphysical journey of enlightenment.

Your Notes:

CHAPTER THREE

A Secret Relationship Between The Earth And Human Beings

Wrapped around the earth is an invisible energy field of electricity and magnetism which is approximately 60 miles high. It is called "gravity". The part of the earth that we refer to as the mantle holds and anchors our electromagnetic fields. It supports the crust of the earth, which is around 30 miles thick, and this crust is what we walk on. The mantle itself is around 2,000 miles thick.

We then come to the core of the planet which is 1,000 miles thick and comprised of two parts: the inner and the outer core. The inner core is a solid mass of mostly iron, surrounded by the outer core, a liquid form constantly spinning in one direction. It is the spin of the core of the planet that creates and drives our electromagnetic fields, which is exactly the same sequence in the way our body functions. This continuance is exactly the same mathematical influence that drives the whole universe and every living species that has evolved. This explains the three dimensions of this planet, where we have just begun our introduction to the sacred codes of the number three. We surmise that it is around 3,030 miles to the centre of the earth.

Now let us take a look at the 60-mile radius of gravity fields surrounding the earth. Could this be 30 miles releasing out from the earth, and 30 miles of mirroring and gravitating back to the planet? This is exactly the same way that the unconscious/higher mind works, as the unconscious/higher mind is the highest realm of our intellect, which mathematically measures every thought that we think. Our body also has an identical effect which we have named our "aura", (aura: energy of our Soul, surrounding every human being; it is our life force).

Let us look again at the human centre core; we are also created in two parts similar to our planet. Our inner core is a solid mass of mostly iron (strength) also our bone matter, and the outer core is a gas created from that solid inner core (emotions). Every time we think a thought it penetrates into our aura, which is the gas that emits from the Alchemy of our own mind. We call this collection of energies the unconscious/higher mind. That outer core represents our energy in motion, and we are aware that the planet works in the same way. (As mentioned previously, the gravity field surrounding the earth is a coagulation of energy—made up of conscious and subconscious thoughts of every living species.)

The teachings of the Shamanic Principles refer to the unconscious/higher mind as the energy that is delivered to us through the Divine Soul. The metaphysical codes of the unconscious/higher mind could then change dramatically to three thousand and thirty, numerically presented as 3,030 or 30 and 30. That is what I call a code. Take this information through to Sacred Numerology, and these numbers inform us that "my mind is my Soul". We repeat "my mind is my Soul" three times, which, when interpreted through the codes of the Sacred Numerology, collects for us the third dimensional mind where once attuned, becomes the temple mind of the Soul.

You may have heard the story of the iron, or "Bja", of man through the explanations of the Egyptian hieroglyphs. The iron represents the core of our being; our DNA is a creation whose composition is identical to the planet that we inhabit. Our inner strength, known to us as our educational centre, has the divine principles seated in the centre of our being. It is the same as the baby in the womb, where the womb holds the electromagnetic fields of the body, for it is the mantle which protects the unborn child. The mind of the child is protected and held in its innocence through the unconscious/higher mind. Our unconscious/higher mind is the sonic sound of the three dimensions of the mind becoming one; another phrase we use for this is the "home of the Divinity of God" or the "Greatest Oracle of the Divine". (Sonic sound: When we raise the level of our thinking and therefore vibration, this is when we harmonize our thoughts with the potential of "the all" the unseen, where the level of our thought creates and manifests into physical reality, matching the experience).

Our whole planet is all one story; it began with one language, and that language depended on the level of its own intelligence for communicating and opening up to the emotional experiences of those who listened first to themselves, and then to others. We learned to feel what we said to one another, and we learned to touch those feelings as they echoed throughout the body—all of which sustained the beating of our heart. With our heart stimulated, the message carried through to our brain! We learned to smell and taste what was right for us, and, as we evolved, we began to learn to hear ourselves. Our five senses began to awaken, as our intuition grew through the self-confidence we began to acknowledge in regard to our self. Our steps forward began to lengthen and grow through the wisdom that we had begun to form within.

Each time your eyes look at another human, you look at a reflection of yourself. Others become a mirror of the thoughts that you have in your mind in that moment, and they relay back to you an answer to the questions of that moment. It is this way for each of us, in order for us to begin to understand our hidden intelligence. As my story unravelled in me, so it will within you, once you can learn the first major step that will allow you to release your fear and become silent in your mind.

You may acquire different emotions through your seeing than I have; it does not matter, as we will all come to the same conclusions and end up at the same gate. Stillness begins in the mind, and it creates an illusion for you to view or mirror towards your thoughts, where you can become more aware of the direction in which you lead yourself in order to inherit your own future.

Your Notes:

CHAPTER FOUR

When We Take The Metaphysical Journey

When we enter into the Metaphysical journey, we can explore the myths and ancient names through the Sacred Alphabetical codes. Exploring the codes of the Collective Consciousness (Laws of the Universe) in regard to the Mayan Oracle, there is a temple near Mexico that many have called the Hall of Recognition (another reference is the Hall of Abundance). Through the Egyptian principles, this is known as the Akashic Records. It also has many other names through the different levels of languages and lands. That temple holds the codes— or the Akashic Records of the mathematical information of our past evolution. The Akasha ("Ark-Ash-Sha") is explained as the exemplification of the sheik, or the elder of the Tribe, which through the sacred coding, is the one who resurrects the self in order to exalt himself up into the inheritance of the higher mind. Throughout the Mayan Philosophies, buried at the base of the Temple, is the sarcophagus of the supposed sun God, Lord Pacal. Let us pronounce the word "Pacal" correctly: "Pha-Kha-EL". Symbolically, this word represents the "father of knowledge". "Pha-Kha-EL", through the Sacred Alphabet, interprets as, "through the power of heavenly ascension my knowledge heavenly ascends through everlasting life".

A wonderful Merlin energy awakens within us on this journey of life, and it allows us to look at the world without judgement; we begin to see what our truth really is – the dances that we co-create behind the veils of how we interpret what we think. Throughout history the sacred coding is automatically registered in our mind and symbolically envisaged as an old man (i.e., Merlin), so that symbol represents the Collective Power that we have encoded within ourselves. This wonderful Merlin energy teaches us how to produce the magic of our own "royal behaviour" – that is, how we are able to achieve our own satisfaction through the feeling of self-love eternally creating and balancing the self. It works with us, not against us!

The Quest for the Metaphysical Pathway: Metaphysics is the

mathematical measuring of the inner balance of the mind, which we call the "Phi" or "Pi". The Quest is one of learning first to silence and then to listen to our conscious and subconscious minds; and, after that, to move up to relying more on the totality of our unconscious/higher mind.

When you bring this education/learning back into yourself, you heal yourself through searching for your relationship between you and your understanding of your Individual Universal Law. This gives you the opportunity to unfold your inner truth. Your truth can only release itself as you accept the responsibility of your own intelligence, which guides the way to your future. Again, only one story exists; it has thousands of different explanations and descriptions. The explanation, or description, all depends on your own emotional responses as to how you guide yourself to discovering your freedom that is still trapped within.

So, if you come to sections in this book that you think do not apply to you, read through them anyway; one day, they will come to your attention—that is the Staff of Life (support of life). You have many facets to your domain, and those facets create your personalities (aspects of self), those personalities become your responsibilities, and they are available to serve you at any given time. (An emotion is a personality of yours or an aspect of self. Your responsibility lies with the relationship of self, through the power of beginning with just one positive thought).

It is not necessarily through reading my words that you will gain knowledge; it all depends on whether you "listen" or "hear" what you have read. Listening attaches itself to our left temple of the brain, where our logic sense or ego, after seeing its own wisdom, brings that wisdom to our attention. We become attracted to this on an outer level. The left brain only registers thirteen words at one time, and it depends totally on our memory banks to support it. That is why we listen through the left ear. When we "hear" the same pronunciation, it is with the total acceptance of our wisdom registering through our emotional responses, which is our right temple of the brain collecting and accepting our thinking. In other words, when we "hear" something, it is fully registered through the energy of the photographic memory, which is our DNA.

The Soul Energy of the Collective Consciousness (Laws of the Universe); is a mathematical program of all that is. The mathematics of the Universe, which can be equated to pure energy, has always been here long before our gestation into human. This Universe and the millions of other Universes have always been in existence as a mathematical equation. In totality, it became the Divine Intervention or what we term as Natural Law; which we now refer to as the Collective Consciousness—Laws of the Universe. Each program has a law that must always balance itself. It is a relationship from God, Buddha, Allah, or any other name that a religion has brought forth for its own understanding, and this transfers back to you from that God, and also from you to that God, or any personal terminology you prefer. This is the evolution of Sages or Prophets through our understanding the Divine Intelligence. That Divinity is the language of the mind, the body, and the Soul transmitting to one another and becoming one; it is the evolution of the neural pathways that connect with one another in the human brain. You are here for your Soul's purpose, with a body of your Divine Inheritance called your DNA wrapped around you. It is the intellectual light from your thinking that is your creation, not necessarily what you do, but rather, how you think to do things. The higher mind is the intellectual light. Through the inner strength that we confidently release through our right brain, it releases the memories that have been genetically implanted into the aura of our cells; from there, it connects through to the inner vision, which becomes the intellectual light of information that the left brain receives. As each human evolves into his/her own emotional heritage (DNA), through them concentrating on their own self-worth, the transformation of each related word mirrors and reflects through that person's intellectual light, and this then returns back into their thoughts. This intellectual light is the compulsive positive energy or irresistible urge that surges through our life force.

The Laws of the Universe answers to our thinking in a balanced way, although in many times it is not always in the way that we expect it to be! Another name for it is Karma, or the "Kha-Rha-Mha", if we explain it correctly, for this goes back to the early language of the Armenians and the hieroglyphs of

Egypt. If we pronounce it in its correctness, it is the cause and effect, or the accidental and occidental; it is the occidental that is the key to your wisdom. Our accidents are what we have produced for ourselves through our thinking. Our thinking produces an energy. For example, anger can build up in negative energy and if not released through reasoning an accident will occur. The occidental is the final outcome of the length of your stay on this planet. The occidental is the light that keeps this planet alive. That gift from the "All That Is", is our attainment, and it is also how we have produced our next moment.

When people are taken abruptly through an accident; they are also living the mathematical program of the inheritance of their family. Over and above that accident is the occident, and the occident is how they created that accident through their mathematics being realigned to their thinking. The occident is another way to explain the Laws of the Universe in action. The mathematical codes have clicked into action and been brought together!

If only we all could understand this area more collectively, we would begin to realize that our thinking is our foremost priority—it is what allows us to theorize and release the Soul's evolution for the whole family. This is also instigated throughout the whole of humanity; we set the wheels in motion not only for our own family, but also for the town or village that we live in. After which, it ventures out to the state, and then to the whole country. We are oblivious to the consequences of our own thinking, and yet, all the time, the mathematics of the Collective Consciousness still keeps adding up our thoughts.

Weather patterns, dis-eases, viruses, and wars are all creations of the atmospheric conditions of the Collective Consciousness; they are the results of the thinking of this planet. This is the "Occidental" of the Collective Consciousness, and we autonomically tap into this energy when we refer to it as "home". The dictionary definition of occident is "a literary or formal word for West". In the Law of Shamanism, "West" is the last section of the Medicine Wheel that we must collect to bring a closure into our mind; it is the foremost evolution of our intelligence. We refer to this as the dichotomy of our thinking, where we bring our mind together for us to substantiate our thoughts, which will create a self-realization or a solid foundation for ourselves in order to understand what we have already accomplished through our lived experiences. The Collective Consciousness relies on that foundation to strengthen itself. From this we ascend to what is acceptable as to how we act to bring both brains into an alignment with each other. The measuring begins to release the mathematics; the Thoth, or Tot, within has awoken. Through the evolution of the myth, Thoth is known to us as the "Architect" or the "Builder". When decoded, the word "mythology" becomes "my theology", which interprets to us as "my way of life".

Our accidents are what we have produced for ourselves through our thinking. The occidental is the explanation, as to how we have gathered and achieved the accident in the first place. It is not only what you have done to you; it is how the Laws of the Universe answer back to what you are doing to you. I like to refer to the occidental as the "messenger", represented as the Pigeon throughout the Laws of Shamanism. With its sonic sound, it hones in on a catastrophic conclusion of thought, and then it delivers the message to our heavenly home, which is our brain. Throughout the Collective Consciousness, no such thing as a "mistake" exists. The pages that follow, one after the other, complete our story of evolution.

Your Notes:

CHAPTER FIVE

The Hierarchical Mind

Every accident or disaster created in any country is a "Divine" message to all concerned intellectually. Watch what your thinking creates for you, and also for everyone around you. This includes what occurs in your own country. A disaster collects itself through the mathematics of the Laws of the Universe—it may be a plane, car, or train crash, a boat sinking or a building collapsing, or as happens in my country, a bush fire out of control. We are a new country here in Australia, so we are still under the banner of the word Resurrection.

To bring it back to ourselves, the Laws of the Universe reflects back to us the results of its measuring in order to show us the direction we have taken. That disaster can be as simple as a broken fingernail or jamming your finger in a door. Even down to which finger was jammed. Was it through your thumb, your **a**ttitude, the pointer finger—your **e**go, the middle finger— your emotional **i**ntelligence, the ring finger— through your relationship to **o**rganize the thought or lastly the little finger—through the **u**nderstanding of what you were thinking? Stop pretending. Notice how each key word relates to A-E-I-O-U, the vowels of the language we speak? This information is recorded through our right brain, we learn this way. The left brain doesn't want to know about it! The ego's learning (left hand) is Attitude, Emotions, Sexuality, Relationship, Pretence!

The Collective Consciousness registers all of our conscious thinking; everything in our body is mathematiszed, all of which must be returned to the conscious mind in order for our energy to continue to grow through the human evolution. Would you like me to start on our teeth? The two top front teeth relate to our attitude. The top row of teeth are how we pronounce our words (metaphysically interpreted, how we think/words). The top row of teeth are further divided from the left front to the left back=ego, right front to the right back=emotions. This relates to you looking out in front of you to gain perspective. The bottom row of teeth represents our rejection of self, our stubbornness. The bottom row of teeth are further divided from the left front to the left back=ego, right front to the right back=emotions.

Step by step we have built up our own demise, and this we must answer to. Bringing this story back inside ourselves can explain it all to us. If we can learn to understand and accept this from within, the only responsibility we have, is to get the story right. That responsibility lies with the relationship of self, through the power of beginning with just one positive thought.

We have the ability to tap into a Hidden God (Higher Self) that is genetically announced within each one of us—one that our two eyes cannot see. The Hidden God remains hidden through our innocence of knowing the self—or maybe it is through our ignorance of understanding how we overprotect our self, or through another of our excuses, such as keeping ourselves locked into what we have already attained, which is our past thinking. Some of us feel safe living in the past, as it deters us from moving forward, and that is okay, but then where is the progress for the future generations to inherit for all concerned? We often rely on the blanket of our fear to keep us safe and warm.

Throughout the old languages, the word "past" means "to Sin"! So when we ask God to forgive us for our sins, are we asking him to forgive us for living in yesterday, or to forgive us for the mistakes that we inherited from yesterday? The word "sin" metaphysical interpretation is: gathering our thoughts about that which we have already lived, and which has now become our past. Now that is worth thinking about. In other words, the Collective Consciousness is correcting me, telling me to stop relying on yesterday's thinking. A new experience lies ahead, but if I sit still in yesterday, I am automatically delaying my next positive moment.

We must learn to serve ourselves in the moment, with the knowledge that, through nourishing and nurturing each thought we think, we are automatically creating our own future. The ones who step out there from the crowd create a world for themselves, and this energy attracts attention for the next one who has the courage, through believing in self, to follow. The same story is how our personalities, which are also referred to as our aspects of self, support one another to exalt our mind!

Our Individual Universal Law expects that as we receive, so shall we give; as we empower ourselves more, this reverses, becoming, as we give, so shall we receive. Empowering ourselves: When your belief in self builds upon its own strength and creates your next positive thought, your life becomes so much easier for you to manage. Are you changing the molecular structure of your whole body by thinking a positive thought in regard to yourself?

Our giving and receiving urges our intellect forward in order for us to move up into the next advancement of our inner-educated intelligence. This is the explanation to the entire collection of religious and mythical stories—for example, the Holy Grail, which is the emptying and replenishing of our own cup of life. It is our Individual Universal Law creating the Laws of the Universe! It is where we all become involved, and, through time and cause and effect, we have created and advanced our evolution for all humanity to inherit.

When an animal completed itself through attaining its own zenith (i.e., had reached the highest level of its own understanding), it could not move forward and act, so over time it gradually became extinct. For heaven's sake! Please do not let this be the same message for humankind! When decoded through the Sacred Alphabet, the interpretation the word "human" is: "The-**h**eavenly **u**nderstanding of **m**astering and **a**scending through **n**ourishing our self". An easier rendition is "the heavenly understanding of man". Always the codes release their strength through different levels. Extinction occurs through the unfolding of the DNA; believe it or not, it is a blessing through the Divine Laws of God, (Laws of the Universe) not a misfortune for us to earn.

Life began with prehistoric intelligence, and through the millennia, each species of animals grew to be huge through having the ultimate consciousness all to itself. Its energy began to collapse in on itself, and when it had reached the outer boundaries of its own development, that development was the result of all that was. It could not move forward and free its own understanding of self in order to ascend to the next step of its own wisdom, as it did not know how to. The species of its Collective Inheritance had not advanced enough to allow this to occur at that time. Its time was up. This gave the next generation of the species—right through to us and beyond to futuristic man—the opportunity to advance upon that previous intelligence, and the results are that man has had to move beyond the previous recognition.

As the next species evolved from itself, it had to become more advanced mentally than its predecessor. This shows us the electrical circuitry of evolution. As one overtook the other's intelligence, it could move forward. This created a space or doorway in the consciousness, and only the more advanced intelligence could step through into that territory. The hierarchical mind (also known as the Higher Self) opened up to its own distinction, and progressive behaviour followed through. The previous species became smaller, through its own belief, and could not extend itself. Einstein's Theories of Relativity at work here!

We have many of those prehistoric animals still living here in Australia, still foraging out in the desert in a minute form that continues to evolve from the original. They now hide under a blade of grass rather than rip off the tops of trees. Why are they still here? They are cold-blooded creatures living off the last of their own evolution, and that cold-bloodedness is the final "earnings" of their own gratification, which comes from the ultimate goals of their Collective Intelligence answering back to them. Their energy becomes more condensed through the maturity of the next species birthing its own, and this is their last stand as a species that they must conform to.

Your Notes:

CHAPTER SIX

When You Learn To Become The Trunk Of Your Own Tree Of Knowledge

When you learn to become the trunk of your own tree of knowledge, you are in total control of your branches. It is how your roots are situated, how you have gravitized your thoughts and earthed yourself that controls the direction in which your branches grow. Always remember to reverse your thoughts backwards: From the tip of the branches, we are the results of the trunk. What emotion is behind each branch? Which emotion is trapped in the trunk? A tree stands still; it does not get up and run away from itself. It must be flexible where it can bend itself in all directions. The conformed energy in the trunk of your tree creates the direction in which your branches must grow.

The roots of trees are metaphysically reflected as the human toes; our toes represent the final outcome in regard to understanding ourselves. In between our toes are the drainage points of our lymphatic system. Please refer to your Reflexology or Zone Therapy manuals to see how important this area is for you to stimulate and drain. Remember, the lymphatic system is our last system that threads its way completely around our body before our birth to protect our internal-ness. Give between your toes a rub every now and then and thank them for the position they uphold in keeping us upright.

Our fingers are the final outcome of our action and how we are acting out our levels of understanding that we have brought together as we mature into ourselves. They are the tips of our branches and the leaves of our own tree of knowledge. Those leaves on your inner tree of knowledge are explaining the emotional intelligence (thoughts) that you are releasing at this time. The top side of the leaf is attracted to facing the light and the underside is quietly in abeyance, for the opportunity to present itself. The top side represents our outer perspective and the underside is representing our inner self. Both sides will become your holographic imprint. The strength of your tree is reflected in every leaf and each leaf represents a page in your DNA, or your inner Bible.

The tips of our toes and fingers represent a beginning and an ending; it gives us the direction of which way the next ley line automatically creates itself. (We have electromagnetic energy ley lines that connect with our internal meridian lines to assist with our human potentiality that are concurrent to the universe).

Every time we are thinking a thought, we need to understand that thought before it can act, otherwise it becomes a re-action. That thought cannot act, until we have released the courage to believe in it. It is a re-enactment; in other words, we are locking it back in. Therefore, we have to re-enter into the act-ment, re-enter into the re-enactment to take that step forward. By re-playing something from the past, we are re-enacting the same old story, and while we continue to do so, we can never progress forward. We are retarding our own futuristic growth.

It is through the belief in oneself in each given moment, that creates your futuristic moments to harmonize and balance the mind to appear before you; where you and your mind become that amazing tree of knowledge in all of its glory to share and have the same experience and thoughts.

Let me explain hologram/holographic imprint

Metaphysically we are indelibly imprinting our own hologram, which begins when the third eye has opened. Our consciousness is comprised within a personal light body hologram which consists of electromagnetic waves. The higher and more powerful your vibrations become through accepting your emotional intelligence and wisdom, the more your waves will have the strength to regenerate the self (string theories are at work here).

For example, when I was in the outback searching for a particular track, through my focused mind I could bring information from "out there, to in here", where it was registered in both hemispheres of the brain at the same time!

I could look through the trees into the distance over the other side of the horizon and just ask what was on the other side. I just had to focus both left and right hemispheres of the brain into becoming one; this allowed the third eye to create the vision that could not be seen in the third dimensional world; through bringing the focus back into two dimensions, one of the moments and one futuristically, everything could follow on from this moment! All combined, this allowed the truth to reveal itself to become the supreme moment and I was able to find the correct track to travel towards.

So, to summarise: Metaphysically, we are constantly imprinting our own hologram through the power of our thoughts, beliefs, and emotions. When the third eye has opened, we are able to access higher levels of consciousness and awareness, and our personal light body hologram begins to take shape. The higher our vibrations become, the more powerful and impactful electromagnetic waves will be.

By accepting and cultivating our emotional intelligence and wisdom, we can raise our vibrations and strengthen our hologram, creating a positive and empowering reality for ourselves. This means being mindful of our thoughts and beliefs, and actively working to replace negative patterns with positive ones.

Through the teachings of the Shamanic Principles consider the falcon's stillness of mind. The falcon gathers its own responsibility and creates for itself a perfect hologram, where it can see through all the layers of the Collective Consciousness. Look at the bird, and you will see that it is able to fly and hold itself in abeyance, while in its stillness, in order for it to be able to mathematically set its prey. All this depends on the power and use of its wings, its inner action.

Your Notes:

CHAPTER SEVEN

The Importance Of Self And The Evolution Of Consciousness

The relationship to the unfolding of our emotional intelligence comes from within our own action. If we enquire of self, for example we listen to our thoughts, correct our thoughts if required to a positive form, believe in our self, balance our mind, become our own stillness, we receive our own go-ahead and our own inner light, through the Hidden God within, to expand our wisdom. It ascended from the Collective Consciousness through its stillness, and this light transfers into us through the cells of humanity in order for us to grow.

We begin to understand the message from the Collective Consciousness when we receive the same message in every cell of our body. As God/Universal Life Force or whatever you would like to term this energy, is out there in the Cosmos, so too does the same mind within us all repeat that God. As we think, so does the Universe measure and return our thoughts. This occurs through our understanding of the autonomic responses of the nervous system, which are the messages sent to and registered by the human brain. We watch the evolution of consciousness expand through the genetic inheritance of human devotion to the discovery and importance of self. The importance of self is a step we must take in order to understand our third-dimensional reality, and this we must learn before the next level can present itself to us.

The stories throughout my books have been told many times before; my version of them may sound a bit different as I explain to you the mathematics of how your mind works on your behalf. Throughout my training I had to walk through the Netherworld for a number of years. That is also referred to as the "underworld" and/or the "worlds of the Duat". Another name is the "pit-Duat-ary" gland (pituitary gland) in the body. These are the laws that represent the "dark night of the Soul", where we are still trapped in the darkness of our own thinking, through our inheritance of our previous generations.

We must search for our intellectual light (evolving our inner light), which will become our protection.

Through balancing your mind, you uplift your emotions, where you become not only more aware of your intelligence; also, more emotionally aware. This emotional intelligence is a reasoning of perpetual motion, which continuously balances and harmonizes your mind, body, and Soul, and which also equates to your family, friends, and country (home). The whole planet has the opportunity of continually harmonizing and reflecting itself back to you, and this reflection is the mind, body, and Soul of all.

How do we balance the mind?

Through conscious awareness of your internal dialogue. Is the self-talk positive? If not, stop the chattering mind (repose the ego). Breathe and prepare the mind by sitting in silence (similar to a reset on a computer). Then focus and use words to honour yourself, allowing the correct thought to come through (use positive affirmations). Be the personality of Self Esteem—Regal—be in your Royalness. Remember you are the most important person on this Earth.

The medical profession knows much about the left brain—or ego—however times are changing, as I have so many students globally who are deeply connected to every facet of the Profession. I watch closely as the medical profession continues to learn how to understand the responsibility and function of the right brain. Why? The left brain reflects through to an outer boundary, whereas the right brain electrically conduits through the resonance—or channels—of our inner emotions. All this places the responsibility inside our head within the middle ear, which must accept, hone in on, and balance that entire responsibility (i.e., the responsibility of our thoughts). The middle ear is a very important set of scales that weighs and measures our thinking. Once these scales adjust and balance each hemisphere with the other, our consciousness is able to release and freely reach up to the next positive thought. It is the responsibility of our evolution to release our thoughts into the left and right brains, which are joined at the stem of our cells research station, known as the pituitary gland. This area of the body is the introduction to us producing our own sonic sound. (Sonic sound: When we raise the level of our thinking and therefore vibration, this is when we harmonize our thoughts with the potential of "the all" the unseen, where the level of our thought creates and manifests into physical reality, matching the experience).

Your left brain—or ego—holds onto your fears in order to support itself! It will listen to these words that I have written for you, and your right brain—or creativeness, which is the introduction into your Spiritual self—will hear the words. Do you understand? All this allows your fears to relax. Those fears have stored themselves mainly in the pockets of your bowel, which is why bowel cancer is so prevalent; we hang onto the past because we are afraid to let it go. We have our future in the brain and our past in the bowel, so we sit on our knowledge, holding it. We become afraid to use our own judicial wisdom when we have allowed our fear to suspend us. Constipation, haemorrhoids and diarrhoea (also spelt diarrhea) are the results of doing this. Constipation is caused by refusing to release yesterday's thoughts. Haemorrhoids are the strangulation of your bowel through pressuring yourself and refusing to allow your growth to expand into your future. Diarrhoea is the result of not digesting or chewing over your thoughts; you have allotted no time to spend with yourself. Every thought you think has "a reason to its season".

If I can help you to understand and accept, where you can act out your thoughts through self-confidence and assurance; we are then both winners. Are you becoming aware of how our inner body is communicating with us through each thought we think? Hopefully you will have the opportunity to rake away your fears, as this is the sole—and Soul—reason for you to be here, where it is what this life's quest is all about, your inner Spiritual Quest. We rake up all the leaves after the autumn season has ended, and we prepare the garden for winter. Winter is the time for hibernation, and it is through our own hibernation that we are given the time to dichotomize, which means to sort out right from wrong and refrain from making the same mistakes. When we look out our window again, our garden looks tidy and free; the raking has allowed it to regain its own silence and to breathe new life as it prepares to birth itself for the next season.

Let's understand this inner Spiritual Quest correctly. You exist and you are here through and for the benefit of mankind. You must learn to think before you do; and, more importantly, you must understand before you act. This thinking world of yours is called your "Essence", or your "Spiritual Self", and that self is here for you to realize the quest of your life. Remember that the word nowhere is "now here"! If we can bring the past into the moment, we can learn to accept it; that moment then promotes through its inheritance the action which promotes our future. Through this acceptance of self we bring both our understanding and action together, which creates an eclectic implosion that begins in our aura, the energy of our Soul. The word eclectic is the higher religious experience automatically forming itself throughout our body. It coincides with the unconscious/higher mind and returns our future back to us. The Spiritual Quest is your life unfolding itself through you looking at you! That is the cycle of life. Everyone is doing this journey whether they are aware of it or not, and that is one of the main reasons why you are sitting here reading this book!

Your Notes:

CHAPTER EIGHT

Releasing The Past, Fears, And Evolving One's Light

There is nothing new on this planet; it is the same story repeating itself until humanity, as a whole understands what has, is, and will become. For a transition to occur an evolution of consciousness must transpire, and in this transition it is important for you to understand that you are the most important person on this Earth. Your individual consciousness (your life force) resonates to all.

We have inherited our DNA from our parents. Metaphysically our DNA is symbolically embedded with the last sixty-four generations of our family, which are the basic building blocks that create our intellect. This DNA is a filing cabinet of history that is comprised of the life patterns of our parents, grandparents etc. It is our foundation. We create our building blocks from this information, as we have 23 chromosomes from our mother and 23 chromosomes from our father, which provides us with 46 chromosomes, and we have the ability of re-arranging our genetic inheritance that has been passed down to us. We can utilize the 46 chromosomes, and use them as our tools to evolve our consciousness.

When we improve ourselves by positive and forward thinking, which is then expressed on a cellular level, there is an opportunity for our DNA to unwind itself (improve one's intelligence). By our stepping forward (positive consciousness), we are also healing our genetic inheritance from our own ancestors. As your knowledge grows, the more understanding you release and expand within yourself. We eradicate the negative layers and build positive layers—our intellectual light advances. When we as humanity utilize positive and forward thinking, this energy is then assimilated into the Collective Consciousness, subsequently opening up another realm of intellect for humanity to use.

Your life program (your life program was created through your parents' DNA, which provided the basic principles for you to become you), keeps on creating itself through each of your thoughts building upon the other, and the transformation continues until you have taken your last breath. That energy force field grows in strength and opens you up into your Higher—or heavenly—Self. That Higher Self follows you through every thought you think, always encouraging you to create and expand your thinking.

To carry your DNA inheritance into your next step of humanity's earnings is how and why you have evolved to be here, clearing your past generations thinking and programming the mind of your future generations. Once we have accepted this program, it is no longer a detriment to your consciousness; the freedom you create in your mind will allow your intelligence to have the ability to evolve even further. Once we have recognized and solved the tasks that have been given to us by our genetic inheritance, we are free to collect more information to add to the benefits available to us beyond this program.

Clearing the Past—Stop stepping back in the past

Do not become bogged down in the past; that song you sung is over. Stay in the moment, as that moment is a reflection of how your future must come to you. When your emotions become bogged down, do not speak them, just be aware of them; look at them, and watch how they begin to accept this new you. Address the situation in the moment, and watch that moment disappear into the next one, and then, as you ascend, all those emotions learn to become one.

It's good you are clearing past thoughts—they are layers of your old limitations, inhibiting your next advancement and the realisation of your Royal-ness. Focus now is on our responsibility of our thoughts to create our life and this is based on our opinion of self. It can't work while you have repetitious thoughts based on past limitation. Clearing ones past generations' thinking can prove to be an evolutionary journey.

How does one stop stepping back in the past?

Until you are prepared to take that first step forward, the

Laws of the Universe will help you to your own expectations; never the less, the moment you put your right foot forward, is the moment when the doors will open wider. Then you must keep on moving, without re-creating that old thought or fear. You will know when you are ready for each new step of your journey; your light within will then open new possibilities and show you the way.

If that same memorial experience or thought is created back into your thinking again, you must stop it before it becomes greater. I still remember my traffic lessons when I went to school: **stop, look,** and **listen**. This was an affirmation I had everywhere in my restaurant to keep me on my toes, when feeling tired. Try to search beyond the moment to see how this energy or thought re-created itself. It is not a learning experience; this time, it becomes an earning. There is a big difference between learning and earning: the former means "looking at", and the later means "looking through". Our Higher Self—our unconscious/higher mind—presents all of these experiences for us. It gives us the opportunity for our thoughts to repeat throughout our life, until we can find the strength to overcome them. One thing in life is certain: You cannot run away from yourself. There is nowhere to hide!

Remember to retain an awareness of your thoughts, sensations, memories, ideas, attitudes and beliefs. Anything that we are aware of at any moment of time, forms part of our consciousness, and becomes our life force. (Consciousness refers to an individual "sense of self" or "inner-self".)

Consciousness builds on consciousness. We often have a stream of consciousness—the flow of thoughts from our conscious mind. Our consciousness develops itself, one layer over another similar to thin layers of silk—all the layers are an active force of energy. Our consciousness grows and connects from these layers.

Also review your dreams. We usually begin dreaming from midnight through to 2 a.m. Those dreams represent the torment that we have created for ourselves, from our past thinking. In the dreams, our Higher Self (unconscious/higher mind) informs us that there is something we must release in our lives through our current thinking becoming choked up with unnecessary chatter; there is something of the past that we must bring up and rectify. For instance, if we are sacrificing to the self (doing things for others and receiving no benefit for self or trying to avoid responsibility for ourselves), that sacrifice will keep us in the past. Release can be found in the act of humbling self to one's Higher Self. When we have accepted these tokens of remembrance, we can thank the experience in order to free ourselves and move forward.

<u>Clearing Fear</u>

Your thoughts are heard right around this planet. The Collective Consciousness sonically registers them. We must remember that our fear, as well as our expectations, creates our reality.

Understand that our fear is with us at all times—until we have earned the freedom in the mind to allow it to release itself. Up to that point, our fear is our driving force, and we cannot live without it. That fear is our ego rebounding back into its own self-acclaim, and, through you accepting your inner equation—or the responsibility that you now understand regarding self—you can see how it manipulates your well-being and how it wants to regain or seize control.

Find the strength to love your own insecurities—your fear, which is the child within us all. That child must grow up—or spiral up—into becoming the adult. The word *spiral* refers to the place where we have the opportunity to turn around and accept our self, at the exact moment when the positive energy steps forward to offer itself to us.

On your life's journey, you will die to, and grow away, from your old ways of thinking. Through your own assertion, you will learn to release your fear through finding enough courage, strength, and power to believe that you are a miracle (a "mirror of your cell").

Always listen to your thoughts. You create your fear in the moment through your thinking. An affirmation to help: "I release my fear and I live and accept this Divine moment in my life."

It was the little things that I began to understand at first, I discovered how to release the pressures of my past that had a hold on me—at last, through my awareness, I could see how my past tried to control me. For me to attain the Avatar education in my reality was phenomenal; there were years when I felt like I was trapped in an iron lung and had great difficulties learning to breathe; as my intellect released itself from my bones. For years my body ached inside me, as I learned to release the fear that I had inherited through the embedment of my DNA. And yet there was another side to the journey I had undertaken and that was of pure bliss for me to release my inner freedom. Many times I felt like I was ten feet tall. As my cosmic force fields extended; which is my auric fields of intellectual attainment I knew that there was nothing the universe could present to me, to keep me embedded in my fear. It is similar to the astronauts adjusting their breathing apparatus when they are out in the ether, floating around in space.

If we do not allow our intelligence to release, we begin to walk backwards, and this sets the pathway to the destruction of what we are innocently aiming for. We lack in our responsibility to earn, which allows our fear to suspend us.

I have been informed that George Lucas, the creator of "Star Wars", undertook training under the guidance of the late brilliant author Joseph Campbell, who wrote more than sixty books and gave us a wealth of information that he had gathered from around the world regarding the "Masks of God'. When George Lucas had gathered his information, he sat down and wrote the magnificent "Star Wars" series that is still so popular today. All his movies can be taken as exercises explaining the emotional personalities (aspects) of the mind, and these personalities are just a spark of what is in each human to view for him/herself. Luke Skywalker had to find his strength in order to release his light, and he did so through overcoming the dark force—Darth Vader. The secret of the movie came that at the end, when Luke found out that the dark force was really his father. In other words, he had the responsibility of clearing his past evolution—or DNA—of its own negativity, and only then was he free to collect what he needed to experience for himself.

Review your dreams—Sleep is needed for our ego—the ego being the world that houses and controls our fear. It is through sleep that the unconscious/higher mind can return to us the results of our thinking. Therefore, we must accept the responsibility for our own thoughts as they are presented back to us. Those dreams come to us in a metaphysical resonance; they are delivered back to us in the form of a riddle or a parable as stated previously. We have to work the meaning of each dream out in our mind.

Dreams also manifest from the stories of our past generations, if our higher mind thinks that we are regaining (using) the same excuse as our ancestor lived. Those excuses are the fears that are instilled in us when our past generations did not understand or overcome their own excuses. Therefore, those dreams bank up in every forthcoming generation.

When we are aware of and can decipher our dreams, we free up not only our own fear but also the fear of our past generations. When you are lying in bed and going to sleep you shut down the conscious self (left brain/ego), then you open up the subconscious self (right brain/emotions) and release the unconscious/higher mind, this world of silence, will be knowable to us and we will know where we are heading. We are participating on this journey of wanting to know what is up above, but the old stuff holds us back. So, now you should be able to understand how so much of your fear has been created.

Our reality is already created for us when we are born, through the thoughts of the mother's ninety days before gestation and also within the first three months of gestation, and by our genetic inheritance. This is your foundation. Therefore, you are born with the foundations of reality on the thoughts of both parents. For example, a son would grow up like the father because he reflected the emotional hiccups that the father had.

A foundational reality is already set, and then it is up to you how we learn to understand who we are. The Natural Law is of who you are and that is your challenge to become who you wish to be. What are your desires? How do you wish to define yourself? You have the ability to overcome, to step forward to release your inner fears. Those thoughts that you think, are they holding you back? You have the right to step forward as your our intellect unfurls.

For those of you who know yourselves, your thoughts are the creation of dreams for the rest of humanity, all through you understanding yourselves. When we are aware of and can decipher our dreams, we free up not only our own fear but also the fear of our past generations.

Our Intellectual Light

You cannot rush this life quest. Listen to yourself and learn to hear, and then, through the process of understanding, it will all be absorbed slowly. Every cell has to be reawakened back into its light, and those cells then have to equalize and become harmonically and energetically balanced.

The Laws of the Universe are involved with you closely as you evolve up to the next step. These Laws do not come down to meet you. They invite you to enter up into their light where you receive the contentment which is called enlightenment to release your peace within. Being enlightened is when the Universe works for you; it is not you working for the Universe, so, through trusting the self, you become your own Master, where you guide your own light.

As per releasing the past and fear from our thinking, have an awareness of your thoughts, sensations, memories, ideas, attitudes and belief in self—discovering the inner you. Anything that we are aware of at any moment of time, forms part of our consciousness, and becomes our life force. As you think positively, your cells vibrate to a totally different frequency, and the molecular structure of your mind expands to create new opportunities. Consciousness builds on consciousness and produces an energy force.

If required, remember the **stop, look**, and **listen** routine as stated previously. Reset your thinking, stay in the moment. A simple way to stay in the moment is to take ten, slow deep breaths. Focus on breathing as slowly as possible, notice the process of breathing.

It is important to learn to be silent within yourself; for, that is when your inner self communicates to you in images through the light worlds. Those light worlds are the illumination of your true self. The only way you can find that light is through the intellectual release of our DNA advancing through how you think. It is the intellectual light from your thinking that is your creation, not necessarily what you do, but rather, how you think to do things. Your Spiritual light grows as you bring the knowledge from that adjustment within yourself, and you realize what you have earned. The word "Universe" means: "to unite the verse", or "to unite the words you think to speak".

The ancient Egyptian Pharaoh Akhenaton through measuring his own mind up into the heavenly energy—or the crown of the head—had opened his heart to himself and was a complete manifestation of God/enlightened. Akhenaton went through his night—or netherworld—in order to find his own light, where he had earned his balanced mind. The Aramaic language has pronounced Akhenaton as "Ayanatun" or "EA-nat-on". "EA's" nation of light.

Through the evolution of the myth, the first city that Akhenaton created was supposedly called "ON". The other was known as "UR", as to how we understand our intelligence and release the freedom of the Divine self. He then went on to build the city of Amarnia (or the "Amen of 'EA'", as the words "Amen", "Amon", or "Amun" all come through the heart when it is opened to the self). This city has been created around the heart area as we look down from above on to the river Nile. Remember the river Nile represents the spine of humanity and Luxor is the navel which houses the universities and temples, where we receive our gestation of intelligence. Hence, when we say our prayers or sing a hymn, we end with "Amen". He was the last of the pharaonic kings to achieve the gift of representing and explaining the completed story of humanity's journey into enlightenment, which many of you term the "afterlife". Do you see how we have collected the information that "Tut-Ankh-Amon" (or "-Amun"; also known as Tutankhamen) became the Golden Pharaoh of Akhenaton? He is representing the intelligence of the unconscious/higher mind—hence, the golden mask. And, if we take a look at the mask that was placed over the young king's head, viewing it from the rear, we see how they have placed the alphabet of both the left and right hemispheres of his brain in blue and gold stripes. As the headdress is collected around the back of the neck, we see how the tail is bound symbolically to represent our vertebrae! It is representing our own DNA, as to how it traverses up into the higher mind. Now that we understand the gift of the Oracle, it has become the evolution for all of humanity to follow "ON", right up to this present day. Or could it have meant the journey of the "Solo-Man", whom we have named Solomon?

When we speak through our heart, we are viewing everything through the eye of the complete mind—our third eye— where we emit our jurisdiction back throughout ourselves! This autonomically creates the intellect we use when we speak with others! Our newly found wisdom will create for us the Pharaoh Akhenaton, the first Pharaoh to attain a balanced mind, through which he was able to enter up into the unconscious/higher home of God. Now that you can understand the Metaphysical language in its clarity, the word "PA'ATON" symbolically represents our pineal gland—or, as it is known through the Egyptian principles, the Sun God "Ra". Through the biblical period, this is where we see through the Eye of God in order to release the language of the Gods!

As the sun is to the Universe, so it is with the solar disc that is autonomically created within each human brain. This light manifests through the release of its own strength as our emotional intelligence unfolds itself. This, through the Egyptian prophecies, is the birth of the "Ra". Our Spirituality is the eclectic light that we earn through obeying this intelligence that we refer to as "home"; it is permanently connected throughout every species on this wonderful planet. It is the conscious, subconscious and unconscious/higher minds working as one.

Throughout the Laws of the Shamanistic principles, we

are asked to use the electromagnetic fields of "Elephant" and "Whale" quite frequently, as their sound waves travel completely around the planet, which adds to our gravitational fields. They are excellent collectors of eternal energy. We need them to fortify our strength; we do not need to eradicate them! Elephant, through the Laws of Totem Shamanic energy, represents "Knowledge", and Whale is "Communication". Their sound vibrates to a very low frequency of around 2 megahertz, and it travels along the crust of the whole planet. Those sounds are collected throughout the electromagnetic fields, which are construed correctly to the given point through the contact of the vibrations coinciding or arching with one another.

Whales create fields of light energy that can be seen from great distances, even from satellites travelling in the outer Universe. That vibration collects, and then it is forced through the next field of energy until it completes a full circuit. That is why both species can speak to the other through their unconscious/higher mind. They can hear each other's thoughts through the sonic sound that they produce, through the beat of their own heart. All species that vibrate to the same frequency can hear and understand this sonic sound.

On a trip through North Africa to Mali, an Elder of the Touaarik tribe (this tribe is also called "Tuareg") gave me a compass that they have used for thousands of years in the desert, in order to travel from oasis to oasis. It is created in the sign of the cross. He explained how the compass works in the sand. The sand reads the shape of the compass, and the priests read the energy waves that the sand creates. The reading is construed through the mathematical vibration of the silica that is produced through the sand, where it releases the light; they explained to me that they were never lost in the desert, as the light always points in the direction of the north. Those High Priests have been looking after the "tomb of the books of truth"—or the ancient Library of Tumbouktu (pronounced in English as, "Timbuktu") for nearly 2,000 years; they still wear the same style of garment and symbols, and they still rely on the compass to direct them as they collect and scribe the ancient languages of the past.

In summary treat your thoughts and mind with the greatest respect. Do not look back on it; but, instead, please learn to look into it. Maybe now we can begin to understand the story of the first Pharaoh of Egypt and why he held himself under his own command. As the next generation of each Pharaoh continued through his own lineage, he learned to accept the other premises that each forthcoming generation could inherit. Until we came to Akhenaton!

Your Notes:

CHAPTER NINE

The Wheel Of Life

Through our Life Program you will have your own beliefs through your religious inheritance or tribal law (family belief system), which has been your understanding since childhood. Your family had an inner yearning to do things right for their own future. I have no intention of interfering with your religious beliefs, and I would never interfere with your tribal law; it is your own way of life. Religion in Latin is religio, meaning "binding oneself to linking back into the Soul". It is also deorum cultus, your culture, your inheritance, the gathering of your eclectic life, which is the result of the seeds your family and ancestors have passed on for you to inherit. The harvest you reap is solely your responsibility.

My grandmother explained to me, when I was a child, that one Wheel of Life existed, comprised of two different-sized circles which held it together, as she had a penny-farthing bike. These circles are the outer rim and the centre, which we call the "hub". The hub, which fits over the axle, has to uphold the weight, and the spokes that we place between the rim and the hub must have the correct tension in order to balance the whole wheel. All religions are the spokes of the same wheel. If one spoke is loose the wheel begins to wobble, which pulls the bike out of its equilibrium, which made it more difficult to ride. Let's remember that and keep this Wheel of Life balanced and always rolling forward.

I remember a moment from my childhood when one of my friends said to me, "I am not allowed to be friends with you, because you belong to a cult." I answered, "No, no it's okay; I don't belong to a cult. I am not a Roman Catholic!" That was the end of that friendship, as she was Catholic. My grandmother chastised me over my remarks and said that my wheel of life was certainly out of balance and that I had to retention my spokes, so that they all balanced correctly for me to be able to move forward. Can you see how we are all endowed with the same thoughts? Ask me what religion I am now, and I will tell you freely that I am all of them. I have collected all the spokes in my own wheel. The Universe is a creation of the Divine, made for all of us to inhabit, and room enough exists for all to have a front row seat!

I take great pleasure in walking into any church, in any country, in order to sit and listen to the word of God. I can do this, as I now understand the emotional kingdoms of what remains hidden within the Soul, and where this opens us up to the expenditure of the Collective Consciousness. Only one story of our evolution exists. It is to the level of understanding that each one of us walked out and saw things through different eyes, searching for our own road to travel down, so that others of same mind could review their own possibilities. This began to rearrange the Divine plan, where we could grow up and learn to release our burdens of fear, or the heaviness of a cluttered mind that we force ourselves to carry.

I think back to Martin Luther, and how the emotional truth that he was searching for, forced him to face himself. The light that he had found within, in turn, allowed others to also release their fear. That not only changed many people's thinking, it also strangled those who were strangling others through their evolution at that time. I can see why around 155,000 people had to die for this huge catalyst to become the next wave of humanity's earnings, all those years ago. (Martin Luther was a 16th century monk and theologian.)

I have my way, and it may present a different explanation than yours. It doesn't really matter, as one original blueprint exists for the whole Universe. So, as it is with God, the Collective Consciousness—or the inner sight of the unconscious/higher mind—all form a coherent creation of our intelligence. It does not judge; it is here to answer back the truth of our thought and balance all. That story is here and available to every one of us; it is hidden within each of us, you see. We bumble and fumble our way through life; we read of someone else's experience; we listen to someone tell a story; we watch the news on TV or listen to the news on the radio that keeps us in tune with what is happening outside ourselves. This keeps us connected to all, and it lifts us up into a higher expansion—or vibration—for us to accept the Laws of the Universe.

CHAPTER TEN

Mythology Is A Coded Intelligence

Mythology is a coded intelligence that is stored in your force fields—now referred to as your aura, or the energy of your Soul. It is within and surrounding every human being; it is your life force. Every one of you will automatically open up and live the Myths of Time—whether you are aware of it or not—which will allow this inner language to release up into your mind as you ask yourself a question. Look at every experience that you complete, and then see the realization of one of the myths handed down to us through time. I took great delight in realizing what myth I was living and also in accepting that it had to play out its role; I could not stop these codes of consciousness before they had finished their explanation to my game.

From the beginning of time, each myth that has been brought forward has been created through a story gathering itself around an emotion, energy-in-motion, that is part of the Collective Consciousness. These myths are explanations of how you can balance your mind, which allows the next positive thought to come through. We receive so many experiences to learn from, throughout our lifetime. Examples of Myths are described metaphorically in the following chapter.

Through all those years of my training in isolation to understand the world of Metaphysics, or the matter of physics, I had an urge to reconnect with my children. When I had finished the journey of those years, to what I thought was to my own and God's satisfaction, I went back, but my children did not recognize the new me. I had been absent for so many years; I ached in every bone in my body, wanting to receive their support. When we met, I spoke differently and with a calmer voice; I also had an answer to all their questions. We had to feel our way around one another again; we had to open up our emotional responses so that we could reconnect and smooth out our seams of love again.

I embarrassed them at times as I opened them up to their

own consequences of how they had protected themselves, busily deceiving themselves through their own innocence. Every answer I gave to their questions ended up as a story, as I had so much information stored within to release. That story was my truth, where I had to enter into the light to find my contentment, and to be able to reach and attain my enlightenment. Their old mother had grown up, and she could not and did not use her same old excuses. I knew I had to walk away from them emotionally to allow them to search for their own truth, which would end up the same as mine, anyway—it would just have a different explanation.

Today I am so proud of my children, as they have proven to themselves that they are in total control of their thoughts and all aspects of their lives. Of course they are accumulating greatness in all their spheres of light. These spheres will collect and come together for them to realize how their success created itself in their future.

My experiences are here to show you how you can bring that belief into yourself, and then allow it to grow through you. That will give you an equitable understanding of being able to claim your own self-rule. One of the first initiations the Shaman has to learn is the art of shape-shifting. It is so simple now that I have learned to master myself. We Shamans become a mirror of every one of you—we become your age, your reason, your answer to your question. Once we have stepped up into our telepathic inheritance, which can only be acclaimed through silencing the mind, we are sucked up into the Collective Intelligence of the Universe, through the vortexes that evolve through the rearrangement of our heart. These changes are created through the current value of our **belief in self**, which has opened up our DNA. This automatically realigns our inner mathematics, to assist us as our truth is revealed back to us!

Belief in self is a fundamental aspect of personal growth and development. Following are some ways you can incorporate into your daily life a belief in self:

- Identify and challenge negative self-talk: Negative self-talk can be a major barrier to self-belief. By identifying negative thoughts and challenging them with positive affirmations, you can begin to rewire your thinking and cultivate a more positive mindset. State as an affirmation "I believe in myself".

- Set achievable goals: Setting and achieving goals can help to build confidence and self-esteem. Start by setting small, achievable goals, and gradually work towards more challenging ones.

- Focus on strengths: Everyone has strengths; it can be anything. By focusing on your strengths and building on them, you can develop a sense of confidence and competence.

- Practice self-care: Taking care of yourself physically, mentally, and emotionally is essential for cultivating self-belief. Make time for activities that bring you joy and relaxation, and prioritise your mental and emotional health.

- Keep "in the moment" and quiet the mind chatter.

My explanations are to explain to you how to listen and then hear yourself through an inner level, in order to prepare you to be able to release your next positive thought. We are given a choice, you know! You are beginning to realize that you are in charge of your mind; your mind is not always in charge of you. This is where you have the opportunity to sow the new seeds of your intelligence, so that you may reap new harvests. You can then gather your own grain (ideas) to nourish and feed yourself. Are you beginning to understand more easily this Metaphysical language? Take your time. It is a language explaining the metaphorical approach to who you are. It makes it easier to understand.

Your Notes:

CHAPTER ELEVEN

Metaphysical Interpretation Of Myths

I have metaphysically interpreted many myths and they are scattered throughout my books. When we read a myth we can look back into ourselves and understand more fully the mythical stories that have been handed down through our generations. In summary form I have included some examples of different myth interpretations in this chapter.

One of the most popular myths is Avalon, especially the myth told in story form of **King Arthur** and the twelve Knights of the Round Table. The Round Table is, of course, inside your head: the table of atonement, or "at-one-ment", is situated under the top of your skull.

I would just like to explain the word "Arthur", and how it came to be. If we go back into the ancient knowledge of language, we find that it means "the art of knowing all, once we open the door". If we bring it into the codes, the word Arthur means "ascending and releasing Thor." The God Thor (remember the Viking mythology) was the voice of the light—or lightning—which relates to the Baptism from God. Pronounced with a silent h, it means "door". So, once you walk through the door, this myth is the knowledge of all. This is where the Knights of the Round Table were able to release and support Arthur as he journeyed into the discovery of himself. Now, what are the twelve knights? Of course, they represent the twelve strands of our DNA, or the twelve Apostles in the Bible that you have earned to support you.

The Lady of the Lake, of course, is the emotional mind keeping the sword (the "Soul's word") in her command. She lives in the waters—that is, the consciousness. Remember that the word is mightier than the sword. The rest of the story is about personalities (aspects of self) that Arthur had to birth in order to bring himself together to become his temple mind. Every story is exactly the same; they had to wander through the experiences of their past to achieve their freedom.

We can only remember the myth or truth of yesterday when we quickly override our negative thinking. It cannot store itself, although, the truth can. It is a pronounced energy that is automatically held through the Collective Inheritance. That is just one of the wonderful stories of how every human can understand themselves. Metaphysically, the sword is the cross we accept—it is our mind. The cross is the light, as well as the shadow self. In other words, when we need our own protection we hold our fear close to the heart. This is number four in Sacred Numerology, which is the temple of self. We are training our self, moment by moment, to have control over our thinking, which explains why the sword is always placed in the right hand. It is showing us that this is our inner action; which can only be achieved once we have opened our heart to release the Divine Intelligence through our selves.

The **Holy Grail,** which is the emptying and replenishing of our own cup of life. It is our own Individual Universal Law creating the Laws of the Universe! It is where we all become involved, and, through time and cause and effect, we have created and advanced our evolution for all humanity to inherit.

If we care to go back a few thousand years to the men of the North in the age of the **Vikings**, we can look at the four most popular Gods in their mythology. I have travelled in those lands periodically, and I have heard many of their myths. They are exactly the same stories as the Aborigines tell in Australia, the land of the South on the opposite end of the planet. These Gods of the North are Wyrd, Odin, Thor, and Frey, and the myths of their journeys and explorations were handed down from father to son, and from tribe to tribe.

Now let us look at those four names—or thoughts—and hear my explanation as to how they have been presented to us. From the word (Wyrd) comes the ode, a poem or celebration, (Odin) to open the door (Thor) to freedom (Frey). Now isn't this what we all wish to acclaim for ourselves? Every human attains a higher consciousness when we have realized that we are the earth, and we are also living the stories that were written before us. The heaven of the Vikings is called Valhalla, which is also known as the "halls that are veiled". We could also pronounce this as the "Halls of Valor". Another explanation is to pronounce this as the "Veils of Allah". Many similarities exist between the Viking myths and the Arabic translations. They referred to the Elders of their tribes as "Urt", and each leader, as he was selected to represent the people, was given the same name. Through the Arabic philosophies, we are aware of the city of Ur, known to us as the lighted one in the Mesopotamian region. The tribe placed their responsibilities onto the Elder, and he was called the "Earth" of his people. Does this word sound familiar?

So it is with every culture of every language. We have a hidden explanation that the unconscious/higher mind exfoliates back into our understanding of our own spoken language, in order to suit the applicability of the thought that we herald in the moment. Everything is measured by the transference that permeates from the energy of that thought. This is the loading zone of the mathematics of the mind.

We now understand more fully that, throughout our past, stories were told of "giants of men"; these were not physical giants, but rather, men who were advantageous in their own minds. This is the language that was available to us throughout the evolution of our intelligence, and once our fear subsided, we trusted and spoke. The Elders had to have the intelligence that the rest of the tribe was afraid to search for. Why? Because they had to make decisions and take on the responsibility of thinking for the whole tribe, which expanded their consciousness—and which was beyond the mind of the ordinary person, whose intelligence had not yet accepted itself!

Three Metaphysical ancient Gods: **"EL", "AN", "EA".** Interpreted through the matter of physics—or the Metaphysical language—these three names are here to remind us that we can attain Everlasting Life, Ascending and Nourishing, with an Energetic Attitude. All this is similar to how we introduced our self into our spoken word, which was released to us through our DNA. The first dimension of God "EL" (Everlasting Life), which represents the home of our ego in relationship to our sexual encounters. These encounters are our basic structure of searching for a placement of our own responsibilities. This is the first doorway to where we connect to our lungs of consciousness, which is where we understand the breath of our inner worlds. Our next evolution is into the God "AN" (Accepting and Nourishing), where we have understood our primordial earlier worlds through collecting our intelligence and accepting the possibilities of harvesting the seeds we have already sown (our thoughts and deeds). You have entered up into your education system, which is your inner university. Automatically, this subconscious awakening brings the information up and through to your heart, which opens you up into a belief that you can accomplish anything your mind desires. The combination of this energy then traverses up to connect us into the highest form of intelligence—our unconsciousness/higher mind—that is, to the Divinity of the God "EA", which, through the earlier language, was pronounced "He-ia" (Heavenly Energy of Intelligence Ascending). This is the last of the three prime Gods that we connect to, and it is the home of our heavenly kingdom, which is situated around the crown of the head. It is where we realize that the Laws of the Universe have a purpose for each and every one of us, and that we all have the ability to reconnect back into the origin of our Soul.

A wonderful **Merlin** energy awakens within us on this journey of life, and it allows us to look at the world without judgement; we begin to see what our truth really is—the dances that we co-create behind the veils of how we interpret what we think. The word Merlin—or, more correctly, as it was collected through the words "Mer-EL-AN", once it was decoded—means that the Meer—or the waters, or ocean of consciousness—of the God "EL" opens up through intellectually nurturing the home of self, which is the mythical home of the God "AN". As we have intellectually progressed through time and accepted the codes, we then changed the pronunciation of the letter a to i. All this means that the "oceans of consciousness" bring you everlasting life when you come home to the inn to rest. In the ancient language, the word inn was originally pronounced as "Airn"; hence, the word bairn, meaning "young child"—or, allowing the self to birth, to be born again. Throughout history the sacred coding is automatically registered in our mind and symbolically envisaged as an old man (i.e., Merlin), so that symbol represents the Collective Power that we have encoded within ourselves. This wonderful Merlin energy teaches us how to produce the magic of our own "royal behaviour"— that is, how we are able to achieve our own satisfaction through the feeling of self-love eternally creating and balancing the self. It works with us, not against us!

The Ancient Egyptian **God Thoth,** who, in Egyptian myth, measures our truth through the explanation of the hieroglyphs of Egypt. Through the evolution of the myth, Thoth is known to us as the "Architect" or the "Builder". When decoded, the word mythology becomes "my theology", which interprets to us as "my way of life". What and how you are thinking right now is the result of what you have become; what you are doing on this journey of life is also learning to understand where you have come from. The abilities and opportunities you have understood so far will determine where you can go on to complete your journey of self-discovery.

Mythology began to explain itself back through the Twelve Houses of the **Astrological Signs**. It is a mirror guiding us up towards the entrance into the unconscious/higher mind. This is where we enter up into the home of the High Priest, the Sage, the Shaman, and the Prophet. They represent personalities that have collected and earned their written stories, as a result of having entered up into these higher territories. We have entered into the realm of non-judgement; which becomes the realm of justice! It is the only way we can enter! Now can you understand the stories from the Egyptian hieroglyphs that are carved on the walls of the temples, regarding Astrology, the language coming from the stars? Once we have passed through the medulla oblongata, we have left our three-dimensional reality—we are living in the afterlife. The Milky Way is symbolically representing the ideas that are available for us to release back into the Universe, all in the service of helping others.

An evolutionary step in the journey is how we evolve into our emotional intelligence, and the right brain has the claim to this fame; it sits on that throne. This is the Divine Myth of **Isis**. In the word Isis, there are two syllables: "Is-is" Decoded, this word means "Through the Relationship of the Intelligence of the Soul". That means that we have to find this relationship within ourselves in order to balance both brains.

You have your own emotional intelligence, and, as this forms and balances, your energy changes through the responses of you respecting yourself.

The **Myth of Cyclops**, which was told to me by an elderly Greek man, whose name was Demos, as we sat together on the seats of an ancient amphitheatre at the back of the Acropolis. He had been explaining to me how they had kept the Acropolis alive for future generations to view. This man had spent his whole life—more than seventy years—working around that sacred complex, and was now selling postcards to the people who had come to his land to see this wonderful place. He explained to me that because the Greek government did not have the capital to keep them employed, the finances were donated from other lands in order for them to continue working.

Tears sprang to his eyes as he explained that during the Second World War, the money that was usually donated to them from other lands was no longer available, owing to it being war time. It was Hitler who had heard during the height of the Second World War that one of the major columns of the Parthenon had cracked and was unsafe and that this column needed to be restored urgently, before the whole temple had collapsed. Hitler donated millions which kept the people in work and food during the restorations over the next three years. We could have lost this important symbol that millions of you have viewed. Demos said that many of his countrymen would bring their wages to help keep them going in this war-torn country.

I know this is a different part of the story than we have been taught, but I also know that it is worth mentioning through my accepting this man's truth. Demos's mind was incredible, he knew every myth, and we spent many hours sharing them with one another. We even had my taxi driver join in on the stories, and he would not leave as the conversation between the two of us was so interesting, he wanted to hear it all. As Demos spoke the myths, I explained to him their hidden meaning through the language of Metaphysics, describing how every myth was an inner kingdom that each human could find within themselves. We became brother and sister as we shared our knowledge.

He took time with the Myth of Cyclops, as it was one of his favourites, and he was pleased when, through me explaining to him the inner language or the hidden messages, what he could achieve and create for himself. Homer explains the relationship to our own inner working domain perfectly in his epic poem, the Odyssey; I pronounce the word "Odyssey" as the "Ode to Zeus" and also as the "ode to see". Remember that the word seeing means "to look through". It is reflected through the right hemisphere of the brain.

One Cyclops was named Polyphemus. He lived in a cave on top of a mountain on an island, and he looked after the sheep. When Odysseus landed on this island with twelve of his men, he brought along a cask of wine to share with the hosts of the island. Do you see the relationship between the stories of Jesus and the twelve Apostles? It is unconsciously relating to us the same story.

Listen to this explanation: Read "Ode to Zeus", and now read "He-Zeus"; now pronounce the first one as "Ode Zoos", and the second one as "He-Zoos". "He-Zoos" is how the Arabic nations pronounce the name of Jesus. Amazing, isn't it? All names have the same explanation! Now back to the story.

On entering one of the caves, which was closest to the shore, Odysseus noticed the huge amounts of sheep cheese and milk inside the cave. He became interested in the size of this being living in the cave, who could consume such a large amount of food, and so he waited for the host to return. When Polyphemus came home and saw the intruders, he imprisoned them and blocked the mouth of the cave. He did not want any intrusion into his life, as he was happy with what he had created for himself.

After communicating with Odysseus for a while, Polyphemus then began to pick up the men and eat them, one pair at a time. When he asked Odysseus what his name was, Odysseus replied, "Noman". Odysseus, amazed to see his group disappearing rapidly, remembered the wine. He proceeded to bribe Polyphemus with the wine, getting the Cyclops drunk.

When Polyphemus at last surrendered to the wine, he fell asleep.

Using a huge staff lying in the back of the cave, Odysseus stabbed the Cyclops in his only eye. When Polyphemus came to, he rushed to the entrance, opening the mouth of the cave and roaring out in pain to the other Cyclops. When the others heard him they screamed out to him, "Who did this to you?" Polyphemus yelled back, "Noman did this to me!" The knowledge that "no man" had done anything to him eased the minds of the other Cyclops, and they returned back to their leisure. This gave Odysseus and the remainder of his men time to escape, by disguising themselves and hiding within the flock of sheep so that they could return to the ship.

Here begins the Metaphysical, where we are viewing the explanation of the Myth of the Third Eye, and the fear that we have regarding our stepping up through our intelligence to open that eye. The sheep represent our personalities/aspects of self, that are still trapped in their innocence; they follow us as we move forward, until they find the strength within themselves to support us. The Cyclops Polyphemus relied on his own innocence and used these sheep to sustain himself. The cheese is the by-product that they, or his own personalities, created for him so that he would be able to nourish himself.

So, as we bring the story together through the Metaphysical, we become aware of why the Cyclops had one eye; this was his inner eye, and we note that he was viewing his world through his unconscious/higher mind. That is why the Cyclops were "giants among men". Shades of Genesis Chapter 6, verse 4, are referred to in this Greek myth.

It is the same with most of us; we use the comfort of everyone else to satisfy ourselves. Through the opening of your third eye, you are being introduced into the world of your inner vision. You are being shown personalities of yourself, and you are beginning to see through all the layers that surround you. These layers, or veils, are your innocence surrounding you, searching for your support.

We note that Polyphemus picked up the men and ate them two at a time. He was taking one for his left brain and one for his right brain; in other words, he was learning to balance his thoughts. Again, the Bible stories are being shown to us, and we are reminded of the story of Noah, who had to gather each animal by twos, and seven for the clean ones—all of which gave Odysseus and the remaining men the chance to hide amongst the sheep, disguising themselves amidst the innocent in order to escape.

You have been introduced into the language of the myth—of your dream world. The unconscious/higher mind answers us metaphorically, where we learn to look through in order to see all things; we are no longer just looking at!

Our Higher Self—our unconscious/higher mind—presents all of these experiences for us. It gives us the opportunity for our thoughts to repeat themselves throughout our life, until we can find the strength to overcome them. One thing in life is certain: You cannot run away from yourself. There is nowhere to hide! Stop your unnecessary thinking when you sense that you are rambling; your unconscious/higher mind is just measuring back to you where your thoughts are leading you to. Pay attention, stand back, and prune the briar—and let the rose come into full bloom.

Now we can look back into ourselves and understand more fully some of the mythical stories that have been handed down through our generations.

Your Notes:

CHAPTER TWELVE

Our Futuristic Time Locks

Only 33.3 per cent of the world's population is capable of accepting the full potentiality of the exalted mind. At this stage of understanding our Collective Intelligence, these are the rules that we have earned from these Laws of the Universe; these rules have collected through the majority of humanity being held back into the old third-dimensional thinking. We enter up into the next level of our education the more we expand our mind; we move up into the fourth dimension, which is the doorway to our unconscious mind/ higher mind. Our layers of confinement are slowly released through the trust we release within our self. The fourth dimension teaches us how we can look through these levels of confinement; or, to explain this another way, how we can look into what we have earned through our wisdom releasing itself. We then tip the scales of balance, and the next wave of 33.3 per cent of humanity is automatically brought forward. They are then handed the same tools that we were given to birth themselves. The stories are still the same. The levels are still the same. The words and worlds are still the same. Remember that the first pyramid was built step by step, and only when it was finished could anyone see the achieved results. Similarly, only over time do we learn how to fill in the gaps.

This next wave is where we step up into our Divine education, which also becomes our responsibility; as we accept our new challenges, we must also help the next wave to understand and act upon their new thinking. As I was told by my teachers, you are here to teach the teachers of tomorrow, not the rest of the world. Their turn will come when their shift of consciousness has earned its next step forward. They in turn will move on and also have the responsibility of the other 33.3 per cent, which will have greater difficulty in balancing what they are incapable of sensing. They must bring their five senses together, and then they will be brought forward automatically, as each new wave of energy evolves itself. Some often refuse to grasp this capability, as they fear standing alone, and so through their innocence they look for security and gather back into the fold. These are also the explanations of the Land of Mu, the Lost City of Atlantis and the New Order of the World, or to be more exact, the Order of your New World.

The lost city of Atlantis means, metaphorically, those people who have not yet connected to the quest of discovering their inner connection to themselves. They are referred to as "the lost cities".

The next wave of consciousness is knocking on the door now, and so we begin again. It is through the understanding of the unconscious/higher mind, which is also the mind of the Ancient Telepathic Inheritance—the Collective Consciousness—that we will begin to accept the possibilities of our future inheritance. All this energy has released itself into the Collective Consciousness over millions of years, and it will be available to all of us as we unfold our DNA, which is our devoted inheritance. This will become our New Order of our New World. It is only when you have looked into yourself that this can occur to benefit you and the rest of mankind as well.

When we have accepted the responsibility of self, our futuristic time locks will automatically open. Egyptology explains this wakening as the opening of the heart, also the measuring of the heart and the feather both weighing the same. Again, our senses assist us through our determination. We cannot remain ostracized from the rest of the world. We are here to adjust our own frequencies and return to help the next wave, this time-shift then evolves 66.6 per cent of humanity. This is where the telepathic communication begins to open the psyche of the Collective Consciousness. Does that number release something in you? The number 666 is what we understand to be the Devil's advocate, and it is through this doorway that we view the truth of all that is. The triple six is decoded through the Sacred Alphabet as mastering the mind—not the mind is mastering us! We view these games of how we wish to try and control others, and that ploy is the cause of our effects—and also the results of our actions.

CHAPTER THIRTEEN

My Journey

I have travelled the world through invitation, and I have explained my story/information in more than forty-eight countries, my books have changed that number to many more, as there are now well over 100 countries that my emails come from, thanking me for my information.

My seminars were addressed in English and an interpreter was utilised in the language of the audience. I realised, through conducting so many seminars, that if I spoke English slowly, many of the participants could understand me. Why? They were learned fellows and professionally minded people who had an interest in regard to learning to focus on themselves; in their silence of listening to my words, they had learned to silence their own mind. The more slowly I spoke, the more childlike my language became. Through this innocence I was lifting them up, automatically moving them up into their next dimension.

They became absorbed in my stories, and many thousands of them have opened themselves up to understand and speak the English language very quickly. I learned that those who had been taught English in their earlier years at school had not forgotten, even though they had not spoken it for many years. The more they focused on themselves, the more the English they already knew released for them. It brought a smile to their faces when they realized that although they might have not used the language, they had not forgotten what they had previously learned—and that is what is most important. The English language was the next stage of their evolution. The English language is the last language to this third-dimensional planet, and it has now become the business language for the whole of humanity. It is from here that we can absorb ourselves up into the fourth dimension.

We refer to the English language as the language of the angels, which brings us closer into the connection of telepathic communication. The Universal Language of Babylon is slowly returning back into our hearts; when we speak, our words are formed on the tip of our tongue. We are slowly coming to the end of our ego, and the higher we ascend, the shorter it should take us to fall. Universal Language of Babylon: for many years, I had been fascinated with the explanations as to how we first began to utter our inner sounds. Where did those sounds come from? How did we learn to hear, accept, and speak these sounds? I learned that the language of the planet had broken up, as human emotional intelligence urged us forward, through our ego enquiring of itself, and that language of the planet became the language of Babylon—to understand the language of the earth. "Bja-ab-EL-on" through the Sacred Alphabet. "Bja", of man through the explanations of the Egyptian hieroglyphs. The iron represents the core of our being; our DNA is a creation whose composition is identical to the planet that we inhabit. "EL": metaphysically interpreted as the first of the ancient Gods—Everlasting Life—Everlasting Life is the Oracle nourishing us through the Divine Oracle nurturing the self. The Oracle: as you speak your words through harmonizing your mind, you release your own Oracle (unconscious/higher mind) and then comes "ON" which is the second city of light, through your oracle returning the nurturing to you.

I began my quest in 1983, and I made a total commitment to God—as I knew him back then—to follow through with the belief that all would be revealed and explained to me in a way that I did not have to compensate through my own misunderstanding of what God is. For the last forty years, after the last of my children had left home to go out and manifest their own world, I have become a research scientist of thought. I was asked to become isolated from humanity, as I could not have any outside information to delete my thought processors as the Shaman—or Merlin—within me, as I began to awaken. This is the difference between learning and earning.

Learning comes from explanations that you receive from the thoughts of someone else. Earnings are released to you from your inner self. We yearn to grow up and are introduced to learning through the education that we receive from someone else, where we are able to choose a career and place ourselves out there for all humanity to view. The earnings come from how we use these educational tools to reach the benefits that we are applying ourselves to attain.

In those first few years I experienced times that were horrendous for me. I was so afraid and alone in the darkness that I had created for myself, and as I grew through understanding this derivative of God, slowly unfolding and revealing the intellectual light that is within, allowing myself time, I saw the magnificence of the possibilities of what we have been given to birth within ourselves.

Over years of experiences, I came to understand my Individual Universal Law. Time is irrelevant to the nature of what we call the mind. The unfolding of the DNA, and the twelfth strand of emotion that symbolically holds together the other eleven strands, was a story that I felt had to be told. The more we believe in our own intuition, the more we are announcing the future strands of our own intelligence.

Let me explain that previous paragraph to you again in another way: I am explaining my story to a group of people who are of many different levels of Collective Intelligence. Over time and through their own influence, they form together and become a tribe; they selectively group into their levels of intelligence, which becomes a telepathic enhancement of one another and autonomically relaxes them on an inner level. As I communicate to them, their thoughts create their understanding. This is their own Bible/Book being rewritten, and that Bible/Book is the library of their future. That library is the culmination of their inherited thoughts, sharing and concurring with the new information coming through.

It is the same with the planet, which has its own Universal Library. These Collective Laws of our planet are releasing the wisdom of all, and we have the same opportunity to release these mathematical laws within us. All of which brings harmony and balance to those of us who reflect our thoughts out into the world, where we can become at one with one another. The more we create these positive changes in our self and learn to support one another, the more information the mathematics of the Collective Consciousness Inheritance will move us in a positive direction.

Peace, love, and light are usually encountered at the beginning of our journey of discovering self, and that gives us the contentment that we crave at that time. That is all very nice, but there are times when that contentment stops, and we are urged forward towards the next hill. "Who is pushing me in the back?" I cried out to God. We yearn to go back to when we felt safe, but we also have to realize that we cannot rely on our past; on this journey, one must always be moving forward. We are the latest species to carry our consciousness for all to hear, and, through our truth releasing itself we are creating the next evolution for humanity to sustain. Be prepared for the next example that the Universe places before you, as you will also be tested; the next step will always be a little bit harder than the one before.

My father, who knew of the commitment that I had begun, explained it to me in this way.

"When you feel yourself falter with the load you are carrying on your shoulders, stop, straighten up, and pause, and then take a smaller step forward. Do not bend backwards or sideways, as this pulls you out of balance, where that movement then becomes the creation of your next excuse. God has his own set of rules, and he does not measure us; we must make that our own responsibility within ourselves; we place that responsibility on our own shoulders; your load automatically created itself through the culmination of your thinking, and it is included in the Laws of the Universe. As you move forward, your heavy load will become lighter, and so the heaviness of the weight is no longer applicable to your moment. Your wisdom then has the opportunity to shine and ignite itself to show you the way."

My father's words were simple and pure, and I had to find the strength to go on when he told me that he had handed his reins over to me. Three days later my father passed on to his next education and died. I have cried for him so many times throughout the years of my quest.

CHAPTER FOURTEEN

A Higher Level Of Attainment And What Is Your Heart's Desire?

What is your heart's desire? Have you come to terms with what you are here to accomplish for yourself? How can we make ourselves feel committed to accept every experience we have lived and more importantly know that every decision we have previously made was right at the time? The wisdom you have learned on your life's journey up to this point is perfect for you.

We all have a deep seated longing to know what our purpose in life is, to help us accept our pathway into the heavenly realms. We can do this while we are right here on the earth. Don't wait until you die. Metaphysically finding our purpose in life involves exploring our inner selves. Here are some steps to help you in your journey:

- Time out: Regular time out, can help you calm your mind and connect with your inner self. Spend some time each day reflecting if you are staying "in the moment" and connecting to your inner self and self-reflection. Reflect on your life experiences, skills, and passions. What makes you feel fulfilled? What are you good at? What brings you joy?

- Intuition: Pay attention to your intuition and inner voice. Your intuition can guide you towards your purpose and help you make decisions aligned with it.

- Dreams: Our dreams can provide insights and reveal our deepest desires and purpose. Keep a dream journal and reflect on your dreams regularly.

- Signs and symbols: The universe can communicate with us through signs and symbols. Pay attention to synchronicities, recurring numbers, and other signs that may be pointing you towards your purpose.

Continuing: Believing that tomorrow is a continuation of today keeps us on our toes, which keeps our hearts open to assist when asked by others. When you have released the confidence in yourself, others will automatically become your own reflection! You are your own maker; remember the only person you have to answer to is yourself! Make the most of each moment and know that you are living up to your own expectations of being completely satisfied. Satisfaction releases courage. Through believing in self, your courage to overcome anything steps forward; you release a sense of freedom you have never known or felt before. All sounds good, doesn't it?

So how does one become accountable to the self with each step of confidence? The most important point to remember is that your life is in your hands, your responsibility lies only with you. There is not one other person who is in control of your mind! It is totally your responsibility for everything you say and do.

Begin by listening to your own thoughts—do they belong to you? Or are you too busy listening to your family or others?

The next thing for you to affirm to yourself is that, in your mind, **you are the most important person on this earth**. Don't waste a moment! Enjoy the freedom of stepping out to enquire of your own intellect; you will be amazed at what it has to offer you. The more confidence you release from within, the more your truth will set you free.

I would like you to feel Lordly and Ladylike with self. You are here to complete an education of discovering this hidden God within, which is securely enveloped within the genes of every individual. You were born this way! Allow it to reign free, to create the miracles in your life that are way beyond your expectations. Enter into the divine design, your space in the universe. Make your thoughts sparkle with light so that your reflection is seen right around the planet.

At one stage in my quest for knowledge, I obtained wisdom from my wonderful time with the Australian Aboriginal people (in my book "Decoding the Shaman Within"). I was under instruction on how to use a particular Shamanic tool, and I was creating my whorls of sound and the pulse and tone to work on my behalf. This energetic sound carried through the outback for many miles, just the same as a drum sends its sound through the bush in Africa, or the call from one elephant to its nearest, as well as its most furthered neighbor. I also noticed in my vision world, that the same sound connected to the ley lines of the earth. This was also heard through the energy of the ocean which was autonomically magnified through the water, which the whales used for communication to one another. And don't forget this same experience is waiting for you, when you have learned to be in control of your thinking.

We have electromagnetic energy ley lines that connect with our internal meridian lines to assist with our human potentiality. The meridians, respond to the energy of the unconscious mind/higher mind relating to the responses created throughout our nervous systems. You cannot see these meridians with the naked eye. They are the autonomic responses of language that flow up through your body from your toes, throughout the trunk and connecting through the heart, where they then flow down through your arms and reconnect back up to the yoke, or collarbone, where we carry and "shoulder" our responsibilities, and then entering up into the temple area of self. As it is written in the Bible, this area is known as the "earth"! Now we begin to add to this information. It is in the neck area where the body begins to enter into the unconscious/higher territory of the mind. These meridians then have to work their way through the glandular system of the neck, reaching up into the glands at the base of the brain. This is our heavenly home, so we are both the earth and the heavens at the same time! You have entered into the home of the sonic sound.

Throughout your life's journey, twelve ley lines will unfold from inside the base of your brain (which begins at the base of the spine), and research explains this as your central nervous system intellectually unfolding itself. This energy is called the "Chi", through the Asian Principles, where it becomes a vortex that you are creating through your positive behaviour, as to how your thoughts begin to collect, where they create a spiral, which continues up into the pyramidal section in the base of the skull. Through this spiral collecting its own life force, it is swept up into the medulla oblongata section of the brain, which symbolically represents the crossroads. Which way do we go from here? Through your twelve strands awakening and supporting themselves, your DNA is unfolding the con-sequences or maybe I should say consequences (two different meanings, one for the ego, left brain and one for the emotions, right brain) of what you have already received through your own achievements. My belief is that when you, stigmata your thoughts with dishonour to self, there is no positive reaction from the brain. Our nerve cells do not react in the same way. When we think in a positive way, the brain has the opportunity to rearrange its own structure, through the input of strengthening the proteins into a multiplicity of ideas, which can assist and promote the thought into reaching up for a higher level of attainment. These twelve strands become your future Disciplines. Read on to discover more.

Mythology began to explain itself back through the years as the Twelve Houses of the Lesser Gods, who would partake of the journey to venture up into becoming at one with self; another influence is through the species that were needed for this transition explained through the Twelve Houses of the Astrological Signs in the stars, as explained through the Greek Philosophies. They are a reflective mirror guiding us up towards the entrance into the doorway of the unconscious/higher mind. This is where we enter up into the home of the High Priest, the Sage, the Shaman, Merlin or the Prophet.

Once entering up into the doorways of the unconscious/higher mind, we have entered into the realm of non-judgement; which becomes the realm of justice! Now can you note a different interpretation in understanding the stories from the Egyptian Hieroglyphs that are carved on the walls of the temples, regarding Philosophy and Astrology, as the language coming from the stars or another interpretation is the light from above? Once we have passed through the Medulla Oblongata, we have left our three-dimensional reality—we are living in what is known through Egyptology as the afterlife, also explained as the fourth dimension. The Milky Way is symbolically representing the ideas that are available for us to release back into the Universe, all in the service of assisting others, who have difficulties in realizing their own truth. That Milky Way is always above us and when we have allowed this information to be heard from within, it will take away the pressure that our fear grasps and holds onto for its own security.

The latter explains the journey into the next world where all throughout these stories of the Apostles, we are reminded of the similarities that were explained in the Old Testament as the Twelve Tribes began their journey to discover themselves. We also read the stories of Jesus and his journey to find his light, as he earned his Apostles, which assisted him to explain our next education. The Book of Revelations brings it all together to coincide with the stories that Egyptology has written for us, as to how we can move up towards the unconscious/higher mind.

Maybe now you can see how the stories are so familiar in both the Old and the New Testaments of the Bible. The former explains the first world, and the latter explains the journey into the next. So, the old Testament metaphysically symbolises the first world, or the first time, it is our past, as to how we began to bring the story together from the structure of Egypt, the stories from the Egyptian Hieroglyphs that are carved on the walls of the temples, for us to learn and then earn. We are still in the process of waking up to this revelation, which is explained in detail in my book "Decoding the Revelation of Saint John the Divine". The New Testament metaphysical symbolises how we move into the unconscious/higher mind.

The history of religion explains the story of the twelve tribes through the Old Testament, and the New Testament explains it as the twelve Apostles or Disciples. Both explain the reason for the twelve strands of our DNA! Don't forget that we also have twelve months that we grow through in one year. So now you can see and understand how the twelve houses of Astrology explain a story that is similar and sometime identical to the books of Bible. Only the language of our feelings has been altered.

The Bible is explaining symbolic stories to you of others,

explained to us through the third dimension; my stories are bringing those stories back into your territory (thinking) and making you responsible for the first dimension through every thought you think; not asking you to run out there and search for something that is already waiting to reveal itself to you from within. I received quite a shock when I was asked to write my books only in the first dimension; as this is updated information that I am revealing to you. This information had to make the reader aware of their responsibility to themselves first, before they could listen to a myth in the making. A myth is explained to us in the third dimension of reality, and an insight relates to the first dimension.

Every change that you make advances your thinking and this corrects the overtone of what you will become in your future. If we brought all this Divinity back into one story, we could understand and watch as the Medicine Wheel creates itself. Take your time and read the words of the Prophet Ezekiel 1—4. The first and second Chapters kept my mind balanced as I read, over and over again, his explanation of the geometry of the Medicine Wheel. Another paragraph that I held close to me was in Thomas 4:11. "He said unto them, 'Unto you it is given to know the Mystery of the Kingdom of God: but unto them that are without, all these things are done in parables.'" This passage confirmed for me, time and time again, to keep on going, to keep on believing in this world of measuring the matter of physics, the world of Metaphysics. The books that follow on offer explanations to you in parables, and, over time, you will awaken your own parable within. Little by little, you will earn the acceptance of yourself.

This journey of life is a quest of the Discipline that one releases unto oneself. Through our genetic inheritance and our life path, we learn to accept and allow our emotional mind to walk before our ego or our fear. We bring the right brain before the left in order to enhance an overtone for us to endow.

Men have a great deal of fear about looking into their emotions—their right brain—while they are on their inner Quest of Life. Women, on the other hand, have great difficulty believing in their own power—their left brain. Both brains are the Collective Inheritance, which is the formation of a lifelong relationship that we create with ourselves.

For one to become balanced, the power and the emotions have to take their seat in the upper house of your own parliament. Evolution is created by you taking one positive step forward, and this quest is one of a bonding of your own relationship through the self. You are urged to come back inside yourself to release this belief; this is how your truth releases and unfurls its flag from within.

Just on a side note I would like to explain why dolphins and whales beach themselves. The ocean species measure with the Collective Consciousness, and, when we are in doubt, they freely return their energy to supplement that same weakness in ours. They follow the emotional ley lines of Collective Consciousness energy, through the awareness of humanity. Do you recall this happening in your area? What was revealing itself to the consciousness that allowed these creatures to step in to surrender their life for the humans in your locale? Do you recall the 220 dolphins and whales that beached themselves off the Australian coastline four days before the devastating tsunami that struck the shores of Southern Asia? The collective governments of the world had reached a zenith (reaching a peak of negativity at this stage) at that time; and, as always, Karma steps in to remind us of our responsibilities. What were the governments trying to instigate in those nations that was not for the benefit of all concerned? This announcement to us indicates the Universal Laws at work!

Your Notes:

CHAPTER FIFTEEN

Stress Levels—Becoming The Boundary Rider

How do we go on...what needs changing, what needs rearranging! Let us start with our self first! How well do you know you? Sit down quietly, close your eyes and look within. What do you see? Focus your intention on how you see the world.

There is a hymn I learnt at Sunday School, "Build on the rock and not upon the sand." The foundations of our home base, must be strong to support the collaboration of our thoughts, whether it be the earth, or our own body (our mind), they must both be respected in the same way. Believe me, when I write these following words: there are millions of thoughts that we release over our lifetime, some are light, others create a heaviness in our mind and somewhere along our pathway a few feel just right! And yet, we forget that our home base has to be balanced to support our weight for us to continue on.

We all seem to be forcing ourselves to exist! Have you ever thought that by giving yourself credit, when it is due, that your whole body opens up as it hears the respect you have in self, through your thoughts and autonomically steps forward to assist you? Please take the time to get to know the inner you, in this way there is no time for your stress to interfere throughout your day.

I want to share with you a story I always explain to my students, when walking into a new area or viewing what is happening in society. It's about becoming the boundary rider. The boundary rider's job is to follow the fence line of large paddocks, looking for holes, to stop the vermin (foxes and dingoes), from killing the young lambs and causing havoc to the rest of the flock. The boundary rider repairs the holes and mends the fence line, which stabilizes the fence until he is satisfied with his work and then moves along the fence line to repair the next hole. He spends weeks out in the paddocks on his own with his horses, swag to sleep in, and cooking his food over a camp fire. When he is satisfied and finished with his job, he can return to the homestead and replenish his supplies and move out to the next area.

These gentlemen are amazing to listen too. They have a story to tell, that is so different to others. Just following that fence line opens up their peripheral vision where they can see through, not just look at, it is through their concentration on the job at hand, where they receive a totally different picture on what they are viewing. Through their focus, their mind has the opportunity to expand on their behalf, it assists them, all through the intention they have in each moment. They receive new ideas, which stretches their imagination and they can watch their plan grow, which have a greater opportunity to manifest itself, than if they were caught up in daily life of being and listening to others. They live in each moment, their focus is entirely in that moment, there is no interference from others, and they watch as their expectations gather a momentum to the end of that thought! That thought is never forgotten as it has been completed. It is always on standby to assist in like-minded circumstances. It becomes an added value to self.

We have to dig deep to find the courage to believe in what we are asking of self. Once we lift the first layer, the second layer has the chance to walk into that empty space, where it is waiting in abeyance to assist us. Keep trying, it's all about you, the stress you are creating, is you lacking in your own security and belief that you can begin to accomplish what you are asking for.

May you all inherit your own breath; it has a myriad of answers waiting to assist you reaching a plateau (a place of rest) in your mind.

<u>I have included a short visualization to release stress:</u>

Imagine yourself on a horse, riding through a beautiful paddock. The sun is shining, and the breeze is cool on your face. You can hear the sound of the horse's hooves as they softly touch the ground, and the gentle swishing of the grass as you move through it.

As you ride, you let go of all the stress of the day. You feel your body and mind relax, and you start to feel present in the moment. You take in the beauty of your surroundings, noticing the vibrant colors of the flowers and the flutter of the butterflies.

You listen to the birds singing their sweet melodies and feel the warmth of the sun on your skin. Your mind expands as you take in the bigger picture of life, realizing that there is so much more to appreciate and be grateful for.

With each step the horse takes, you feel a sense of peace wash over you. You realize that this moment is all that matters, and you let go of any worries about the future or regrets from the past.

As you continue to ride through the paddock, you feel a deep connection to the horse and the natural world around you. You feel grateful for this experience and the opportunity to release your stress and expand your perspective.

Finally, you return to the stable and as you take the saddle off the horse and start brushing the horse, you are feeling refreshed, rejuvenated, and ready to tackle whatever comes next, knowing that you can always return to this moment of peace whenever you need it.

Your Notes:

CHAPTER SIXTEEN

Understanding The Value Of You

When do we begin to connect to our inner story? Usually, it happens when we cannot hear our own thoughts, and so we search for a quietness of the mind, or we try to create a peaceful existence to quiet our incessant inner chatter. Peace filters throughout your body when the mind is quiet, and it comes into contact with the highest essence within you. We feel and become more emotionally aware. Peace has the opportunity to be realized through unfolding its intellectuality, through the ego and emotions harmonizing and equalizing through one another, although not necessarily with one another. Inner peace is our solace which creates its own ether, where it can spiral throughout the brain to connect up into the Alchemy of the unconscious/higher mind. It is important for you to understand that this failure of self over the years still has the opportunity to surrender—to allow you to re-create the old you to an evolved you. It is never too late to change your mind. All of which occurs through you releasing your old thoughts and fears, your ego, and all those old blocked emotions that you have carried with you for your support. To create positive changes in your life, you will learn to accept a more advanced responsibility for self. This is where you have the opportunity to revisit, to be born again, to reincarnate—or to rebirth into yourself—these are the three dimensions of Buddha, Allah, God, etc.

Your quest on this journey regarding earning the inner secrets of your life is a quest of you discovering and understanding the value of you; to place a value on yourself means that you are searching for the importance of your worth. You learn to respect yourself through the feelings of your own values accomplishing their own results, which support you, and you learn to stand taller as you walk through your genetic inheritance.

That is the key not only to the Spiritual Quest but also to the Quest of Life in general. You have the power to overcome, to be in charge of and to listen to every thought that enters your mind. The difference is that you must learn to be still and become silent in the mind in order to hear these thoughts. The only way to think clearly is to think in freedom, and through being free your stillness creates a responsibility that you learn to adhere to. This is the beginning, and it is one of the hardest lessons of life to overcome.

Each question that you have, has its own answer; if you can only learn to trust in yourself enough to allow that answer to release itself, it will do so. Have you ever stopped thinking long enough to hear your thoughts? How many words did you think? Where was your attention focused—on the sentence or on the number of words? When you ask yourself a question, and you allow the next thought to respond to it, you must also allow those two thoughts to collect all by themselves and filter through your mind. Try not to fight it; be totally aware of every thought that you have allowed your thinking to create on your behalf. Let each thought that you hear transfer—or "transverse"—itself into the appropriate position that you feel you are lacking within yourself. Through this enterprise you have given yourself the opportunity to prepare your conversations with others.

If you do not have the confidence in yourself to accept this new thinking, your next moment will repeat itself, and you will live the same excuses over again. Until you can rectify your old ways of thinking through the words, courage, hope, trust and belief, each day repeats itself from yesterday. You are understanding the cycle the Laws of the Universe. When we have understood and accepted an answer, it freely releases itself. It is a memorial death which pulls us up automatically to the next level, and our life then empowers us into our next worthy experience.

If you have difficulties with accepting the previous paragraph, learn to take note of your dreams, which are explaining a story back to you regarding what you are doing to yourself, and which are defining for you your own Divineness. Or, rather, are you watching how quickly your imagination looks for another excuse? This is the explanation of the Oracle. The Oracle of Delphi is the Divine Principle answering back to your thoughts. When the mind is chattering away on our outer boundaries, we cannot hear within, so we search for the wisdom through placing our responsibility onto someone else. This releases the build-up of pressure in the moment, and guess what? After all these quandaries of trying to prove to you that you are wrong, you still have not learned your lesson; so, through God's laws or the Laws of the Universe, the same story must be reflected back to you again and again. My understanding came quickly when I asked myself a question; after I asked, I reversed the question and spoke it back to self. The answer appeared. For example, "Lose self-doubt" when reversed becomes "Doubt self and you lose." This was how I learned to realize that the unconscious recognition of self was communicating back to me telepathically through the inner language that we are all born with. My mirror was reflecting the light of my own knowledge to show me the way.

The myth explains the Oracle in many ways. The carvings on the walls of Egypt explained to us that the feminine is on top of everything, as she is the creator of the garment we wear (symbolic of the thoughts of self). It is through her tutorage that we learn right from wrong. And in all things, remember that it is always a woman who interprets the messages. Why is this so? That woman is representing your emotional mind, and this is where our right brain has the gifts that we are all searching for. This is the beginning of our Divine Inheritance, nurturing back to our logic intelligence. It is where we learn to bring forth our truth, which is buried deep inside the cells, and also through our previous generations having lived their lives in a way that was equivalent to their own expectations. We are layered with the fears that they never had the opportunity to release. This is what we call our DNA, which is our first lesson in understanding these parables or mythical stories. Some say that our DNA is rendered 90 per cent full of useless information. Well, please step up here with me and take a look, and you will find the answers that totally reverse this data. You will find that 90 per cent of this inherited information remains hidden from humanity, which still does not understand this information in regard to the inheritance of themselves! To read the myth is to hear the story on an inner level and explain it back to your childlike innocence. Children can hear the hidden message or understand the fairy tale, and they accept their responsibility with much more fervour when they hear it coming from you.

This journey is yours and cannot be given to anyone else; the responsibility is yours alone. The hierarchical mind, also known as the Higher Self, will always be there to step in front of you, protecting and holding you firmly when you cannot believe or when you have lost your trust in you. You must learn to bring your inner worlds out, and that is how your own Individual Universal Law begins to form. This journey is a very self-centred pathway, where you can share your thinking with others; but, for you to begin to understand the importance of this service, you must remember that you are answerable only to yourself.

This quest can take you a lifetime, and the time it takes depends entirely on the belief you can inherit within yourself. It can also be the time of your life! I laughed myself through many years of my life as I regressed back into how I had used nearly every excuse in the book to ease a moment! Many pathways are out there for you to choose from, and your Individual Universal Law will guide you. That depends totally on the personality (aspect of self) is in charge in the moment, as it echoes out to others. It can become the most powerful world tour you could ever wish to inherit!

Your Notes:

CHAPTER SEVENTEEN

The Master Gardener—Chen

I would like to share a story with you; this is about a day in China that I will never forget. While walking through the avenues of the bonsai gardens with my guide, Chen, I had the pleasure of meeting the master gardener. (It is interesting to note that the Chinese, like the Aborigines, address you by your surname. Why is this so? Both cultures have already evolved up into the Divine language of the unconscious mind!) Back to the story! This master gardener had been working as a caretaker in the same beautiful garden for more than ninety years. He began his apprenticeship at four years of age. In all of those years, he had never taken a day off from his work; he explained to me that he had a responsibility to his "children"—which were these magnificent trees—as they were beings lesser than he, and so he must nurture them so that they could find their own strength. He taught them how to talk to him, and he encouraged the stimulation of their mind, through tipping and pruning their branches twice a year—once in the spring to prepare them for the summer, and once in autumn to help them prepare for the winter, as this stimulated and educated their life force. In regard to humanity; we must also turn and face ourselves at these same times each year and are termed "turning points".

It took a period of twenty-eight years for this master gardener to finalize his apprenticeship, after which time, he could take full responsibility for his work and not have to rely on others' judgement. His training was the same as his own master's had been. He had promised the trees that he would be there for them, that he would talk with them and share their responsibilities. Some of these trees were many hundreds of years old, and yet they still survived in these small clay bowls.

As I looked into his magnificent eyes, he related his stories to me, all the while gently touching the old tree that he was working with. This tree was the oldest in the gardens; it had only the shell of its trunk remaining, with one small branch that had five leaves poking out at the top, and was around nine inches high. According to its chart, this tree was around 1,100 years old. My heart shattered into a thousand pieces at the love that poured from him as he spoke his words. His own family had come and gone, and he was all that was left, so now he could devote the rest of his life to attending to his Spiritual family. My goodness! I could see how his strength had released through his power coming together in order for him to achieve his self-acclaim.

I did not want to walk away and leave this beautiful man; I realized that I was in the presence of a Master of his own wisdom. As I bowed to him and brought my hands together, I blessed him and thanked him for his time.

Chen and I walked away, and, as I dried the tears from my eyes, I felt ever so humble. Chen's arm slipped through mine, as I was teetering along the path, and he said, "Let's go on to the teahouse and have a small pause." As we walked along, I listened to Chen humming to himself, and I noticed that he would repeat the same sound over and over again. I asked if the song was an old one, and he smiled at me, saying, "No, it is not. It is I, calling myself back into harmony. Some of my 10,000 personalities (aspects of self/thoughts) need attention, but they are of no consequence in this moment, so I am informing them that we will share with one another at a later time." My heart melted when I heard his words. How precious to be able to communicate so honestly with the self! What an easy way to be in control, to de-stress, and to release the pressure of the mind—all at the same time! It is so simple, isn't it? We Westerners still have such a long road to travel!

Turning Point: Through our allotted time, a self-awakening (review) automatically happens twice a year. In March through to April—it is known as the "Ides of March". One must turn around and face up to the responsibility of oneself! Again it occurs in mid-August through to September, when it is known as the "Winds of Change". Through the Laws of Shamanism, we refer to both of these stages as the "Turning Point". Every human has the opportunity to turn and face themselves (metaphorically); once after our summer months, and once after the winter, to review our life and face up to the responsibilities of self that we have forced ourselves to overlook.

Your Notes:

CHAPTER EIGHTEEN

Personalities—Aspects of Self

During this interview—or internal view of self—you will get in touch with your cellular inheritance. The human body has a symbiotic structure of cells, and when we can accept and understand the codes of the Sacred Numerology, we realize that through the language of Metaphysics (or the matter of physics), they are a symbiotic interpretation of our 144,000 personalities (aspects) of self. Each one of these personalities is also represented by an emotional thought which is controlled through your ego and released through your emotions. Which one would you prefer?

The written word, spoken through St John the Divine, explains to us the codes of the Netherworld in the Book of Revelations, which is a collection of the stored fear from your past generations. If we look into Chapter 7, verse 4, we read that, from the twelve tribes of Israel, these 12,000 children, which are the next thoughts available to us, would be saved or sealed as the servants of our God in their foreheads. This automatically multiplies the original 12,000, and those numbers then add up to symbolically explain the 144,000 personalities of self. Therefore, an emotion becomes a personality of yours. St John the Divine is explaining to us in regard to you and your thoughts. This Chapter echoes out and becomes the illusion of the beginning of the Old Testament in Genesis, Chapter 49, where Jacob announces to his twelve sons the Prophetic Blessings of the Twelve Tribes.

To become your own master, you must learn to be aware that those 144,000 personalities of self are always listening to you. When you are in your stillness, you must also become aware of which part of you is calling for attention—which part of you is lonely, happy, sad etc. Those personalities are the awakening of your cellular memories. These are the Cosmic Codes of the Laws of the Universe, and each one of us is a flower waiting to bloom.

As this story unfolds, you will realize the power of the minds that have walked before you; they set us an example through these numerical codes. The Egyptian and Mayan Oracles are a perfect explanation. These numbers of 144,000 were carved into the foreheads of those two wonderful figures that we have discovered from the past: "Tut-AN-kh-Amun" and "Que-ts-EL-co-at-EL", which still hold the same codes that were carved into the foreheads of the children of Israel. (Please hear the pronunciations; they are explained further on in book VII, "Sacred Alphabet and Numerology".)

Also in Revelations 14:1-3 it is written: "And I looked, and lo, a lamb stood on the mount Sion (Zion) and with him one hundred forty and four thousand, having his Father's name written in their foreheads. And I heard a voice from Heaven, as the voice of many waters, and as the voice of a great thunder: And I heard the voice of harpers harping with their harps: And they sang as it were a new song before the throne, and before the four beasts and the Elders: And no man could learn that song but the one hundred and forty and four thousand, which were redeemed from the earth."

These verses are explaining the culmination of your thoughts, and they are an introduction into your inner strength through your heavenly kingdoms welcoming you into your discovery of your own Kingdom of God.

The symbolism of the lamb is you in your innocence, and Mount Sion is the human brain. Let us look at this word "Sion". Through the Soul's Intelligence, the Oracle Nurtures; this is an explanation of our first City of Light. The earth is your body, and when you take an interest in discovering the inner you, you become your own land! If we say the word earth through humanity's past inheritance, it was pronounced as "UR-T". The word "Urt", through the codes, means "understanding and releasing the truth". It came as quite a shock to understand the wisdom of these equations, which all came about through my spending seven years of my life in reading the Bible from the end to the beginning—from Revelations back to Genesis. One more thing to understand before we move on is the word for our ultimate Truth, and it is pronounced in the German language as "Neu Troya", which means "New Troy". It is an extension of one's intelligence, through the understanding of the original word "Truth". We now look at the wisdom of the word. London was previously called New Troy, which meant "New Truth" or "New City of Light", and was then transferred into L-ON-DON ("El-On-Di-On"), meaning "everlasting life is the Oracle nourishing us through the Divine Oracle nurturing the self". It is how the left hemisphere of our brain will take notice of the right for it to continue. Remember that the word "ON" is explained to us through the mythical stories as the "First City of Light".

Now we understand the Principles that England must adhere to and live up to. London was originally called the New City of Light, and that puts a greater onus on the Collective Inheritance of that city. We are learning to understand the stories that were written and carved long ago for us to follow – for our own future inheritance. The messages continue to take us deeper into our emotional mind, and remember that it is the responsibility of the right brain to release the truth to us in regard to understanding ourselves. The people that conquered England had found a new home. Was England known as UNG-land, ONG-land, ANG-land, or was it Engel-An-Di? By whom and how was this place first pronounced to us? Which part of the original Babylon did the conquerors and the conquered evolve from?

Let us return to a previous passage, and I will explain it in a language (a "land gauge") that you can understand. "And I looked, and lo, a lamb stood on the mount Sion (Zion) and with him one hundred forty and four thousand, having his Father's name written in their foreheads." As with the two previous examples of Tut and Quetz, we look at the codes of Numerology and explain that this series of numbers is a language referring to the temple mind: The numbers 144,000 interpret as "I am the relationship to my temple; my temple is my Soul mind." In other words, you are being informed of the responsibility that you must abide by for everything that you say and do.

Years ago, one of my teachers said to me, "You are your own factory; you are the chairman of the board and have the opportunity to hire 144,000 employees." Now, if I am going to run my own business, I have to have some kind of plan in my head as to what I want to return to the general public to be able to stake my claim, so I start off small, and, through earning my own wisdom, I expand and employ more staff as the business begins to prosper. I must make sure that all my employees are satisfied with their working conditions, because if they are satisfied, and I am in my balance, I will create my ultimate success. I must not play one against the other; I must become my own government. Then, as the employees start to show me what their capabilities are, I can move them up to their next level, which will become an added benefit to me.

Of those 144,000 personalities of mine, there are 72,000 that belong to the dark (ego) side, which is my left brain, and 72,000 that belong to the light (emotional) side, which is my right brain. Can you now understand how we collected and created the 72 names of God?

Your 144,000 personalities are your inner emotional worlds, and they are all instilled with exactly the same information; it all depends on their prowess and how much confidence they have in themselves as to how they apply themselves to you. You, the owner, must learn to talk and walk these experiences inside yourself. You will become aware that, as your 72,000 light personalities release their belief and move forward, the conversion of the dark will automatically change to help them release their fear, so that they are free to move forward. This is the logic mind and the creational mind working as one. When there are an abundance of orders coming towards my factory, I will realize that these 144,000 have balanced through the victory of the chairman of the board.

When you can begin to accept your hierarchical mind within, you learn not to judge with the two eyes on your face; you have allowed them to lead you to this point, to attract what you see in front of you as an illusion of what you are viewing. Your third eye reflects up into the forehead, and your visions become your inner sight; this eye creates its seeing by looking through all the divisions of your confinements, which becomes the reflection of all the layers of your inner Cosmos. Now you can understand why we dream! Your eyes are closed when you sleep; therefore, your ego is in a state of rest so that the message can be transferred back to you, where there is no judgment available for you to use.

These Cosmic Laws have no excuses; they do not lie, bend, or waver. They have only one direction, and that is up! The more your belief in self is ensured, the more solidly each one of your personalities will surround you, and these are on standby to support you.

Your Notes:

CHAPTER NINETEEN

The Laws Of The Universe and Promotion In The Workplace

Thomas stopped me in my tracks while I was on my way for a quick bite to eat. "Hi Omni how are you? I am on my break, would you like to share a little lunch with me, and I haven't seen you for a long while?" He asked. I thought for a moment and liked the idea and replied "I only have half an hour Thomas, if that suffices then I will say yes to your invitation." I realized he may have had a question in the back of his mind and I also understood that if we crossed paths, then it was for a reason. I have these favorite sayings like "The more we give, the longer we live." He lived a hectic life style and didn't have much time to spare, so to book an appointment with me would have been difficult for him. Thomas is involved in the high finance market, so it was mainly numbers that were running through his head, not the alphabet. In other words his mind was focused on other things besides his own reasoning. I understood that this request of his was one of his top priorities to his world of thinking at this time. I had known him since he was a child and I have watched him grow up over many years into manhood.

We sat down with a delicious hot cappuccino and waited for the club sandwich to arrive. I placed two cubes of sugar in mine and began to stir slowly. I needed an instant hit of recognition to self at this moment. I was trying to relax and take sustenance and sugar has this element we all need, on such occasions. Sugar comes in and harmonizes self, while salt balances the outer self. I always took both with my meals. I realized I would have to open up the conversation so I began with, "How are you going Thomas, and how is this important career that you have undertaken faring with you?" "Oh Omni, you have hit it fair and square on the head," he said.

"I am coming to a point where I am aware that I am bored with my work. It seems to be the same thing over and over again and it is becoming repetitious, there just isn't any motivation for me anymore. I feel like I am being pulled down and things are becoming heavier to handle. I am trying to seek out a promotion at the moment and I don't know where to begin. Do you have any advice for me?" He asked so meekly.

"Are you asking advice from your work colleagues or your next in command, Thomas?" I asked.

"Well no, not at the moment, I feel like I am stewing in my own juices and also this request for promotion is just beginning inside me," he replied. So, in I went with my Bio Sociology training. "Why don't you start with self first Thomas? How much time, have you given yourself lately? How can you come to terms with your thinking that you have justified this position you are already in? Is there any more that you can do to satisfy this position you were given in the first place and more importantly do you feel that you have carried it out to the best of your satisfaction? Have you thanked yourself Thomas for the education you have received by taking on this position?"

"My goodness, I have never thought of it that way, where are you coming from?" Thomas seemed surprised. I went on to explain to him, "You are your own Universe Thomas and it is most important that you satisfy yourself first through all of your reasoning exemplifying itself. If you are not satisfied, then you will have to wait for your appropriate moment to present itself to you again. Your thoughts will just keep on collecting in uncertainty because you have not come to a final decision that you have the right to control your own thinking. Try not to let your thinking control you or overpower you. We place our self into a quandary when this happens."

"Good Lord, go on, I'm listening to you," he spoke softly. I replied to him, "There is a Law of the Universe, Thomas and every human is in its force field whether they want to believe in it or not. It is what creates the gravity fields on the planet. It keeps us anchored to the earth otherwise we have a tendency to allow our thoughts to run away from us and our final decision we make becomes harder for us to accept. And this Law is available to us all, when we ask ourselves a question; we just have to learn to read the signs. The only way we can do this is to understand our own thoughts. To accept this Law we must open up our own Universal Law to acknowledge and understand the consequences we are busily creating for ourselves.

And we have the opportunity to do this through the courage and belief we find within ourselves. We become more intellectually aware that we are a derivative of our own self importance. In other words our challenge is for us to realize that we are the most important person on this earth. This selfish attitude shocks us into a self gratification. Through this self gratification we are then able to turn our attention around through our own satisfaction and be available to help others who are less fortunate than ourselves."

Our sandwiches arrived, so the next few moments we were taken up with our mouths full of this wonderful crisp salad and fresh crusty bread. Thomas was taking time to think over the advice I had offered. He looked up towards the ceiling as his thoughts began to collect. I felt the mastery of his mind bringing him to a point of satisfaction. He was searching behind his wisdom and this automatically brings us back into our past, where we have the opportunity to review our thinking honestly.

"My God, this will take time and I cannot make this decision too quickly, until I have registered what you have said. I feel you have placed me into a position that I must think my way out of it," he said to me.

He worked in the money market and this profession has a way of tying us up to be available to others. The business mind is something we earn and emotions and our ego have no place of importance when there is work to be done. We are spending our time focusing and measuring our ideas to make others feel important. They are paying our wages, so we feel obligated. Did you realize that money creates excuses for our emotions? Our ego feeds off this energy so when we are depriving our inner thoughts, we spend more of our valuable time trying to endow our self upon others. Also we have a tendency to forget our own personal gratification. We have deprived our own emotional self of its own priorities and we miss out on our future opportunities. Yes, that is a bit of a shock to our thinking, isn't it?

Our time was up and I thanked him for lunch and we both rushed back to fulfill our role in the workplace but two weeks later Thomas rang and asked for an appointment after work and I agreed. He came into the office with a broad smile. After our pleasantries he sat down and wiped my office desk with the sleeve of his suit coat and seemed to remove all the hidden dust that was on the table and said to me. "Oh boy, have you provided some food for thought. My mind has been like a bee hive. I never realized I had so many thoughts just running around in my head endlessly searching for their own compatibility. And I would like to share with you that I think I am ready now to make myself available for the next promotion that comes up in the office. I will wait and see just what comes up. It sounded strange to my ears at first that I had to thank myself for my earnings up to this point. This is not the ordinary run of the mill stuff. And now I know that I have done my best for the position I have held for these last two years. My impatience is over, thank you Omni for your time."

I went on to explain to him that not only had he come to terms with his position but also to accept that the department would notice the change in his outer energy. Our thinking registers with the Collective Consciousness of the planet, and all of the people with whom he worked with, would subtly become more aware of his positive behavior over time and pay more attention to him in the future. We call this the Law of the Universe. One month later a huge bunch of red roses arrived in my office with an envelope attached with a bank cheque for my fee inside and a big thank you note. More to my satisfaction there was also a new business card with his new title of "Manager" emblazoned in embossed lettering.

Take your time to thank yourself for the position you are fulfilling to humanity. You are a very important person and this role you have taken responsibility for, will be a benefit for you in the future. Others will become aware of your possibilities when they are searching for someone to share some of their responsibilities. Become an asset for your workplace and enjoy the job at hand.

Summary

Start with self first. How much time, have you given yourself lately?

How can you come to terms with your thinking that you have justified the work/career position you are already in?

Is there any more that you can do to satisfy your current position you were given in the first place, and more importantly do you feel that you have carried it out to the best of your satisfaction?

Have you thanked yourself for the education you have received by taking on the current position?

You are your own Universe; therefore, it is important that you satisfy yourself first through all of your reasoning exemplifying itself. If you are not satisfied then you will have to wait for your appropriate moment to present itself to you again. Your thoughts will just keep on collecting in uncertainty because you have not come to a final decision that you have the right to control your own thinking. Try not to let your thinking control you or overpower you. We place our self into a quandary when this happens.

There is a Law directing this Universe, and every human is in its force field whether they want to believe in it or not. It is what creates the gravity fields on the planet. It keeps us anchored to the earth otherwise we have a tendency to allow our thoughts to run away from us and our final decision we make becomes harder for us to accept. And this Law is available to us all, when we ask ourselves a question; we just have to learn to read the signs. The only way we can do this is to understand our own thoughts. To accept this Law we must open up our own Individual Universal Law to acknowledge and understand the consequences we are busily creating for ourselves.

We have the opportunity to do this through the courage and

belief we find within ourselves. We become more intellectually aware that we are a derivative of our own self importance. In other words our challenge is for us to realize that we are the most important person in the world.

Take your time to thank yourself for the position you are fulfilling to humanity. You are a very important person and this role you have taken responsibility for, will be a benefit for you in the future. Others will become aware of your possibilities when they are searching for someone to share some of their responsibilities. Become an asset for your workplace and enjoy the job at hand.

Your Notes:

CHAPTER TWENTY

When We Ask The Universe For An Answer

When we ask the Universe for an answer to a question that seems so important to us and nothing seems to eventuate, we want to know why we are being ignored. Why is this question so important to you right now? Are you aware of the consequences that you are predicting for yourself? In our state of awareness, we must learn to accept the good, the bad, as well as the indifferent. They are all connected to the many personalities of you that have recently learned to accept a sense of responsibility for themselves. By connecting to your awareness on an emotional level of "why can't I receive my requests?" Disappointment quickly sets in. The reason for this disappointment is through you not being ready for the expectations (or exaltations) that you are trying to acclaim. Come back to your moment. Breathe deeply and silence your mind, It is not your turn yet. Your question in its impatience to rule, has placed a boulder on your road ahead; in other words, it has climbed over the boulder, instead of you earning the patience to remove it! There is more to learn and earn regarding your question. Start again and rephrase your words, which will rearrange the order of your question. Remember, all will be revealed to you at the right time!

The Universal Law expects that as we receive, so shall we give; as we empower ourselves more, this reverses, becoming, as we give, so shall we receive. Our giving and receiving urges our intellect forward in order for us to move up into the next advancement of our inner-educated intelligence.

As you begin to believe in yourself, your Soul gives you never-ending gifts of knowledge. To believe in yourself takes a tremendous amount of courage, and that courage will lead you into other parallel worlds of existence. Those worlds align within and open you up to your inner worlds, where you have earned the freedom to use them to promote your tomorrows. Parallel worlds are created from your intelligence; they are your personalities (aspects of self) co-creating an experience using a different emotion, and they live deep within your auric fields. They are your thoughts co-creating themselves, which gives you many opportunities to choose your thinking wisely, where one world can autonomically lead you into another. The following paragraph is an example of the gift of learning from the Soul.

Body Language—The Itch

My training into body language began through the teachings of the Shamanic philosophies. My training all began with an itch. An itch is an irritation reflecting out through the senses to connect with its outer boundary, which is the surface of the skin. It is given back to us from the thoughts we are busily creating and thinking within. Instead of scratching myself, I had to learn to touch the itch no matter where it was situated (the importance of where it collected throughout the body evolved later)—and I also had to learn to say "thank you" to the itch. I had to surrender to the itch, brush my hand over it, and pull it away from my body. Lo and behold, once I learned how to do this, the itch stopped! What was this? It seemed so simple and easy. Where did it go? How did it dissolve? Did it transfer itself elsewhere into the body? My skin began to repair itself once I accepted and understood this unconscious reaction, which became a lesson I never forgot. In other words, my thought was being mirrored back to me. I began to realize that I was communicating with another realm of my intelligence. I was stepping up into the language of the unconscious/higher mind. The itch was a result of running the same old movie of repeating the thought (negative thought/irritation from a past event), over and over again, and I would not let it go. Hence, an irritating itch was developed on my skin as I was afraid to step out of the past and clear the thought (until I realised). Over the next few years, I learned to understand every cell in my body, its program, and what its responsibility was to keep me moving forward.

By coming back to the point of your existence, you must learn to release the thought of the moment; Shamanically, we refer to this as the "Cosmic Death", which is just a movement of time that has equalized itself! The word "death" means: the Divine "EA" (or metaphysical third ancient God) of Truth. It used to be known as "Dea-at"; now that sounds similar to the Egyptian word "Duat", doesn't it? It is the Soul's purpose to be here on the planet, and each Soul must release and improve the energy that has collected from the past. We are asked to live and discover this inner truth that is embedded in the depths of the Laws of the Universe, which are also embedded in each one of your cells. We have evolved for a very special reason. You are not just here to issue to yourself an added mistake on your own tribal/family behalf.

Your Spirituality is not just something where you say, "Oh one day I must pay more attention to myself." Your Spirituality is your essence; it is your energy formulating your wisdom. In other words, it is an eclectic invasion of your proprietary earnings. It takes time to accept this information, and it takes time to receive the benefits that this information releases back to you. Never doubt your endless possibilities.

Meditation teaches us how to be still and focus our minds. The Bible teaches us to meditate on our thoughts to bring the mind back to our attention. It teaches us to search for our temple mind, where there is no need for the mind to wander alone outside its own restrictions, which it has formed to support itself. Meditation is also a form of you sacrificing your fear, which allows your freedom to release from within. So, says the ego, "Meditation is an excusable religion." The Western word for meditation is prayer; we were trained as children when we went to church to learn how to ask God for what we could not achieve by ourselves—and to wait for the answer. Allow the different facets of yourself to mirror into what you want to achieve, and then create it for yourself. A meditation can be a quiet walk in the park, sitting quietly looking out of your window relaxing; anything that quietens the mind.

As you evolve each day, your intellect is measured throughout these cosmic laws and more importantly through your own heart. It is the learned respect for self that changes the beat of your heart, which dilutes the fear that has trapped you all of your life. The experiences that you learn and earn each day create your life on this planet; this collects within and automatically creates your own Individual Universal Law.

You cannot just learn your journey, you must earn it, and you earn it by listening to yourself through the acceptance of living up to what you have understood in regards to this revealed information.

The Laws of the Universe are what has been created to arrange your way of thinking through keeping you standing upright, and your own Individual Universal Law is the way you react to that. We are each our own Universe with our own Individual Universal Laws, and we exist within a greater Universe that has its own proprietary law as well.

Let me explain that through a story: You and I are in the same room where you are learning to balance both brains and accept yourself, and I am also doing the same. So you and I, being in the same Universe or room, find a way to search for a compatible resonance with one another. Just as the sun and moon relate to one another in the sky. As you spin through the Universe in your own orbit, and I spin in mine, our paths cross every now and then. My orbit is my own energy, and your orbit is yours, yet we learn to live in the same room. We both learn to accept one another.

It is like a relationship; although it is not a "coming together", it is just a "being together". This allows us each our freedom to be our own individual self. When we turn our attention to one another, this freedom begins to change, and responsibility starts to gather. As our orbits begin to connect with one another, and as we connect more closely, our energies coincide and gather to become one. As that moment passes, our paths separate, and then we learn to refrain in order to allow ourselves to connect back into our own existences. We use the Divine Principles that are embedded in our DNA, which allows us to not interfere with one another. When two people are compatible enough to form a relationship, another law creates and forms itself from that compatibility. We are all different, yet we are all the same.

Your Individual Universal Law is the internal aspect of who and what you are—your true inner self—and it is also the capabilities that previous generations have handed down to you, or gifted you with. You create your Individual Universal

Law through the evolution of yourself, and then you learn to adjust your law to the Laws of the Universe. Your Spiritual light grows as you bring the knowledge from that adjustment within yourself, and you realize what you have just earned. The word Universe means: "to unite the verse", or "to unite the words you think to speak".

Before you judge outside yourself, you must first learn to bring all of that judgement within and look at yourself; look at what you think is your own truth. Emotional intelligence grows from the collection of your positive thinking realigning itself. Open your heart to yourself first, and then it will automatically open to everyone around you. Each time that you breathe in and say, "I am as God is"; you become more pronounced throughout the Laws of the Universe. Just like dipping your right index finger into a glass of water, which we know changes the molecular structure of the water, so are you changing the molecular structure of your whole body by thinking a positive thought in regard to yourself!

You cannot fly high if your wings are still dragging on the ground. You cannot sail the "ocean of all that is", if your anchor is still caught up on a rock in the sand.

Your Notes:

CHAPTER TWENTY ONE

The Inner Kaleidoscope

Our third eye opens us up into the quantum of mathematics where it becomes the mind's eye, where the information is heralded down to us in an ancient language that we learn to understand. When our third eye expands, we see everything layer by layer; viewing this through the brain coerces and magnifies our inner sight. As your intelligence awakens into its new dawning, it is automatically lifted up into the next realm. It reflects a stimulated light to show you the way. As your confidence in you surges forward, your third eye begins to open and expand until it becomes a much larger vortex of light. It becomes the inner kaleidoscope which multiplies itself as each new facet finds its own reflection; this reflection creates a mirror image which yearns to release your truth to you. Your truth is the result of your past inheritance; this is not necessarily known to you on a conscious level; it presents itself through the subtleness of the subconscious energies, which are the emotional responses of your forefathers and—mothers—where the mosaic of the mind begins to create the missing pieces, which brings your life into attracting an abundance of energy.

All of these pieces are then reflected throughout this light and are collected mathematically and brought up into the combustible energy of your unconscious mind/higher mind. To help with this endeavour, we find that our heart beat changes its frequencies as it rearranges the dichotomy of what we were, to what we are now accomplishing in our new-found grace. The more the heart beat readjusts our thinking, the more our character of self ignites. As this travels up towards the base of our brain we find that the restriction lessens around the thymus and thyroid glands, which changes the octave of our voice. This area is known throughout Egyptology as the bands of peace. Again, we can see the colour of this light when our eyes are closed, is a soft hue of blue—a rebirthing of self—and it is permanently switched on to help you see through your darkness.

I would like to bring to your attention a synopsis of my writings, as I reveal to you, how I was trained to exuberantly bring forth my understanding to earn the metaphysical reply to the language of the hidden word of the Collective Consciousness/Laws of the Universe. In Ancient Egypt the hidden one was originally known as Amon Re, throughout the Egyptian Philosophies; who supposedly represented the light or the sun and the hidden God within. This is the intellectual light which is exuded from the pineal gland situated in our brain. When we understand these philosophies in the way they were first described to us; we will realize that their philosophy was initiating us into understanding how we are connected throughout, as to who we become, so that we could learn to accept the unconscious recognition of our self! Please remember my previous writings that the codes of the hieroglyphs on the walls of the temples in Egypt, pyramids, obelisks etc., are explaining the evolution of our central nervous system travelling throughout our glandular systems.

We understand now, that the pineal (Pine–Al or oil) gland, also known as the third eye, is the symbol that the Egyptians created when explaining Amon Re. The pineal gland has what looks like an eye on top of the gland that can only look up! What is this eye looking up at? There is a gene above the eye that is of extreme importance, known to us during our training as the God Head, (now reverse it and what do you come up with? The Head of God). This was also referred to in the past as the Lighted One or the Hidden God. The shape of this powerful little gland resembles a pine cone from which it derived its name. The pineal gland is located in the epithalamus, near the center of the brain, between both the left and right hemispheres, fitting snugly into where the two halves of the thalamus join. It is the final adjudicator of our third dimensional mind, before we enter into the fourth dimension, which leads us into the doorway of our unconscious/higher mind.

All of these stories are explaining the responsibility that both the left and right hemispheres of our brain must finally adhere too. This support naturally balances our thinking as to how the DNA releases our next positive advancement. Our advanced computer is ticking away through every thought we release. These thoughts are being placed in the correct formula where they have been brought together through the glandular system, up into the hypothalamus gland where our mathematics keeps adding and subtracting autonomically on our behalf. The information is then passed on to the master pituitary gland, to be delivered correctly to the appropriate sections of our left or right hemispheres according to our truth; if it is our truth then the information is passed on to the pineal gland, if not we will be haunted by our self through the detriment of our ego, to relive the same experience again, until our ego submits and we get it right! All of which allows the gland to automatically release the chemical substance melatonin, as its secretion is dictated by light. We know now that our light is our intellect mastering the thoughts of the moment, which creates an essence that realigns our alchemy, as well as to reimburse our nervous system.

I feel that this sacred area could be where our dreams manifest, as these two elements of this important gene known as the Head of God and the pineal gland come together to register our truth, to inform us through our vision worlds of the direction we are leading ourselves into!

The Laws of the Universe are involved with you closely as you evolve up to the next step. As previously stated these Laws do not come down to meet you. They invite you to enter up into their light where you receive the contentment which is called enlightenment to release your peace within. Being enlightened is when the Universe works for you; it is not you working for the Universe, so, through trusting the self, you become your own Master, and you guide your own light. This light is the intelligence of your Oracle. So be it!

In reference to the third eye and the insect world I have been informed that a fly has an average of 4,400 lenses in each of its large eyes, so these complex lenses provide fly the opportunity to watch 4,400 repetitions of what it sees holographically, and it all fits, like a giant jigsaw puzzle, into one big eye. It can see through all boundaries. If a fly has a small sense of smell and a large world of vision, why does it sit at the door waiting to come into the house? How does it know when I am cooking cabbage or carving a roast? It is through that holographic seeing that it can bring the mosaic together of how it can read the combustible aura massing its energy from the source of species. It is not the smell—that is secondary. It is the power of the energy that emits from the roast of the aura that attracts the fly.

Welcome to the world of all insects. They hone in on the sonic sound, which means that they all live in the unconscious recognition of the Collective Consciousness. They view their surroundings, and are able to evolve, only through the myth of what has already been created through the evolution of their own purpose. If they can accomplish their status in this world, so can we.

In my research I took particular notice of how the insect population created their colonies through the mathematics that each species had evolved into. They were such tiny creatures who had condensed their energy into so much power through time. Their mathematics had delivered them into their own species through the generations of their ethereal emotions that they had collectively inherited. I realized that we as humans still have a long way to go.

I was fascinated with how insects used the four elements to create the inner workings of the beehives, the air conditioning of the termites, the insects that relied on the trees for their dwelling, those that bred on the water, and then there were those who relied on the air for their continuation etc. They had earned their intellect through having relied only on their own microscopic worlds. Their DNA has completely enhanced itself! They owed their survival rate to the combustible energy that they have evolved into, as well as their ability to sense through their holographic make-up of their eyes, which is how their repetitiousness produced the facets for them to telepathically hone into their food supply; this is also identical to how our third eye teleports the information and is able to communicate with us.

In this moment as I write this chapter, I recall a memory from a long time ago of a bite from a small meat ant on my big toe—the pain went up into the crown of my head and I felt like I had jumped through the roof. That small injection of concentrated toxin stayed with me for weeks. So, next time you are injected by a mosquito, bitten by an ant, buzzed by a fly or stung by a bee, they are answering to the reflections of your thinking. Every consequence in your life is through the results of your thinking; all of it mirrors back to you, every moment of every day.

Allow me to further explain about insects. Each species that has evolved on this planet is recorded in our cellular memory. Insects rely on their sonar, as they do not eat matter; they remove and digest only the juices. They represent the alchemy that we produce in the brain; these are resonances that we collate through the two holes in the roof of our mouth. Through the Shamanic "Totem" energy of all, the ancient species that have evolved before us, represent an emotional inheritance that we can rely on to sustain our moment. They will become the beneficial advisers to help us with our own intelligence when our mind is in the field of doubt.

A metaphysical interpretation of the Ant and the Bee.

ANT—Work

The ant species have the largest brain of the insect world, and therefore have the opportunity to enhance their memory just like the whale an elephant do. Ant has huge eyes just like the fly, which form a holographic view of seeing everything in a multiplied form. This holographic view gives them the benefit of reading the combustible energy that is released from food and is then registered through their antennae, which are their sensory glands. They receive and transmit responses of energy from a distance. Ant can lift twenty times its own weight, so responsibility for self is a must. An ant does not eat solid food; it squeezes the fluid out, drinks the life force and then throws the rest away. That nectar rearranges its alchemy immediately allowing it to open itself up to achieve more of its own cellular memory of its DNA.

BEE—The Gift

Bee is extremely powerful. When Bee enters your life it means an end to ordinary things, as Bee signals the doorway into the "Royal Approach to Self". Bring yourself up into your hierarchical truth where you become a glyph or symbol that creates its own sound, a sound that everyone can hear unconsciously. Once your insecurities have diminished the "Nectar from the Gods" is yours.

The Bee's sting is created from its collected alchemy, which can become a hindrance to others. Poison is released from the unconscious/higher mind and rids the self of insecurities. Like Ant and Fly, Bee hones in on energy and collects only the essence of all things. Bee is an insect of pure mathematics, which conforms into the geometry in our lives. Symbolically this is one of the highest orders that we can achieve. Bee has the wisdom to create the "Nectar from the Gods" and its honey is needed by all the insect population to harmonize and balance their own survival. Bee, in Shamanism, is adding to the evolution of all insects, where the mathematics is now changing into the algebraic and geometrical equations.

Your Notes:

CHAPTER TWENTY TWO

Opening The Heart

The more advanced our emotional intellect becomes, the more we learn to communicate through our collective worlds, which is how our words implode one after the other. Our five senses (sight, sound, smell, taste, and touch) open up as we begin to accept ourselves. These same five senses then begin to create a measurement which enables them to square with one another; very soon they created a resonance of mathematics (thinking vibration) which collects one sense with another, as to how they brought forth the distinction of what we refer to as the "sixth sense", which is the entrance to the doorway into the unconscious/higher mind. We have entered into a new world up here, where there are no excuses, no hesitations, no blemishes of thought, where we have the divine will to go on. Our heart is open forevermore. It does not matter what your field of expertise is, you can be the butcher, the baker or the candlestick maker; it is how our thoughts become congruent with one another that the scene resets itself. All is revealed when our mathematics have proven to themselves (obtained a resonance), where our belief has equalized within our body. We can create our own geometrical light waves and our energy multiplies itself times three. This releases the endorphins throughout our glands where our brain waves begin to speed up our energy.

In reference to the ancient Egyptian Principles the Pharaoh Akhenaton (who built the city of Amanea, or Armania which is situated exactly where our heart is placed in our body) through measuring his own mind up into the heavenly energy—or the crown of the head—had opened his heart to himself and was a complete manifestation of God. Akhenaton went through his night—or netherworld—in order to find his own light, and he had earned his balanced mind. The Aramaic language has pronounced Akhenaton as "Ayanatun" or "EA-nat-on". "EA's" nation of light. Akhenaton was the holiest man of all, shown through the hieroglyphs, writings on the temple walls; he became married to himself, and, when we look at the shape of his body, we see that he is symbolically representing half woman and half-man. Through him measuring his own mind up into the heavenly energy—or the crown of the head—he had opened his heart to himself and was a complete manifestation of God. In other words, we are being shown how he had brought a resonance of both left and right hemispheres of his brain together. To further explain the ancient Egyptian journey of opening the heart, ancient Egyptian royalty wore different crowns/headdresses and the metaphysical passage can be decoded through the hieroglyphs. Ma'at, with her wings outstretched symbolically represents the mathematics of the mind. In other words, she is representing the one who has opened their heart to understand themselves. Referring to the Divine Myth of Isis, in the word Isis, there are two syllables: "Is-is" Decoded, this word means "Through the Relationship of the Intelligence of the Soul". That means that we have to find this relationship within ourselves in order to balance both brains. We begin to earn the strength of our heart when we enter into this kingdom, through entering into and opening up our right brain. These are the worlds of our emotions or our "energy in motion". We had evolved and grown through our confidence expanding, where our education entered our mind and we began to believe in this new form of self. Through the mathematics accumulating within our thoughts, we enter into states of enlightenment where all our feelings release through the heart. More information regarding Egyptology comes in further books.

Through the principals of Shamanism the bird evolution lifts us up into our angelic nature through the opening of the heart. The dove represents the codes of Shamanism as it relates to the gift one gives oneself. This species is informing us always to honor our self! I love to hear them first thing in the morning, cooing to remind me to thank myself for the day ahead. Have you noticed the stain glass window in St. Peter's Basilica in Rome, where the dove is rising towards the light? This area of the Vatican is explaining the heart. Another inference in many cultures is the tiny hummingbird. It is a complete miracle that can create forty strokes of its wings in a single second. Its colour creates its own luminous light through the arching of its responsibilities, which also creates a humming sound that is automatically attracted to our unconscious/higher mind. It lives on the essence of flowers, which is the ultimate code of angelic resonance at this time in our evolution. The hummingbird makes its nest by combining its own spittle with spider webs, which both come into the divine equation of self. Hummingbird multiplies its energy to such an extent that while flying it completes its task in seconds, not minutes. Through its swiftness, the Collective Consciousness attracts itself to the energy it creates; therefore, it lives in perpetual energy in motion. It is known through the Laws of Shamanism as the "Carrier of the Web of Consciousness".

Whales create fields of light energy that can be seen from great distances, even from satellites travelling in the outer Universe. That vibration collects, and then it is forced through the next field of energy until it completes a full circuit. Whales can communicate with one another through their whale songs and through their unconscious higher mind. They can hear each other's thoughts through the sonic sound that they produce, through the beat of their own heart. All species that vibrate to the same frequency can hear and understand this sonic sound.

I love to explain our holy grail as balancing and harmonizing our mind, we can store what we understand about our self, until we feel free to act upon it. That Holy Grail (cup of life) always pulses in tune to our heart beat. When our cup is filled with knowledge, it is important that the information is distributed out to attend to those personalities of our mind (aspects of self), that are still locked away through not being able to breathe their own breath; which again is all through our ego refusing to release its hold on its old playground where it felt secure.

The next evolutionary step is how we evolve into our emotional intelligence, and the right brain has the claim to this fame; it sits on that throne.

Your Notes:

CHAPTER TWENTY THREE

Masters Of Time

In our innocence of understanding ourselves, as children we begin through giving the Laws of the Universe names like "fairies" and "elves"; these are the "little people", and they are little ideas coming together. We then move on to the angelic realms, where these little people grow into becoming our guardian angels. As our intellect arcs itself higher, they become our Archangels, or Ascended Masters, which are sacred arts of lifting your thoughts up into a higher understanding of self. Once understood, we then move or migrate into another higher language, where they are sometimes referred to as the "Ancient Astronauts". As you can see, the little people have grown up and are now a Cosmic example of an intellectual energy force that has collected itself! Once your confidence becomes more self-assured through understanding this explanation, you will be well on your way to becoming aware of your God-ness within. I like to refer to these symbolic energies as my "Masters of Time"; they are explaining the stories that the previous generations have handed down to me as my inheritance—part of our Collective Inheritance. So come along with me, and I will introduce you to the next level of humanity's earnings, which will connect you to your availabilities, which are still trapped beneath the layers that you have kept contained through your innocence.

Those Masters are connected to your higher thoughts; they are forms of energy that we communicate with twenty-four hours a day. They are our thinking processes, and, believe it or not, they are the fibres of our nervous systems, our glandular responsibilities, our muscular vibrations and pulses and toning; and all of these are the communication channels that allow the Alchemy that we produce to create the functional responses to the brain. They are how the human body evolves itself. They are the hidden language of communication, which has collected through the ancient laws of the Divine Equation, and those laws are embedded in every one of our cells.

So, as the child grows up through believing in angels and

becomes the teenager, we also excite our own nervous systems enough, through becoming the Warrior, to reach up and expand our own consciousness, where we begin to collect to the myth. The nervous system works through to our glands, and these glands become our Masters of Time. They are the introduction to our sonic sound, and this, my friend, is what I am trying to explain to you: It is the ultimate language of the unconscious/higher mind.

The higher your emotional intelligence releases, the higher the Master who presents itself to you will be, until you become the master of your own consciousness, which is your destiny. Once you have attained this level, you are given the royal birthright to plug into the all that is, where you can view through your inner eye the wholeness of the Collective Consciousness. The more that Higher Self of your intelligence unfolds, the more focused and disciplined you autonomically become, through understanding and accepting your ethereal thinking! We all have this Supreme Being embedded deep within us, and we understand it to be God. It is humanity's birthright that this Hidden God becomes available to us all, as we unfold the layers of our past. Through our being deprived of our freedom—through our fear innocently keeping us locked into our past—we have become blinded to the possibilities of seeing our future, and this has kept us in our own bondage for most of our lives. As our intelligence unfolds, we focus our attention back inside ourselves, instead of placing it on others (i.e., outside ourselves).

During this process, we have a tendency to alienate ourselves; this is where we have the distinction to rely more on each decision we endow upon ourselves. We build up our confidence as we project a positive outlook, and this can only come into its own through the revelations of our truth in all its supremacy, believing in all that stands before it. Only when we have unfolded ourselves do we have the right to offer ourselves to others; this is our life's education. When we have earned this freedom, others will look towards us for the answers they seek to their own questions.

You receive to the level of your own intellect, as described in Matthew 7:7, "Ask and it shall be given you; seek and ye shall find; knock and the door shall be opened unto you." This wonderful Scripture—remember that is Matthew 7:7—brings us to discuss the number seven, which is denoted through Sacred Numerology as the Christ Consciousness. There are two sevens here, and the number two is denoted as the word relationship, so the message is explaining to you that you have formed a relationship with your inner light! How many of the clean beasts did Noah have to collect? How many seals are there to open through the book of Revelations? Read on; it will all be revealed!

Being silent means you allow the Higher Self, to step through these layers (your layers of consciousness) which you once had to support you—to lovingly protect and nurture you—and, through that achievement of stepping through, you open up to becoming your own light. This light is the intelligence of your Oracle. Just a slight mention here on two words, look and see. We "look" at things, using the left brain; we "see" through things, using the right brain. When you are in your stillness, you have the opportunity to be more aware of everything that is going on inside you. Do not put yourself on a cloud, where you are floating out there somewhere towards the next planet. You have to come back home; your gravitational forces need your attention. Your old self and your new self are on the sacred pathway of learning to become one.

The first step to understand is that we complicate ourselves by allowing the ego to force us into a competition with our inner and our outer worlds, while we are learning to bring both hemispheres together. When our ego loses its control over us, it become confused, and it tries to regain its own superiority.

The right brain is not in competition with the left while it views its own illusion; it has the patience to wait for you to silence yourself, so that it may enter into the inner furore in order to be heard. Likewise, the left brain is not in competition with the right while it views its own illusion; but, you are now advancing into your own territory with new ideas, which disturbs the left brain's comfort zones. Your new creation of thought comes through those two hemispheres of the brain respecting each other in silence, or reverence, which solidifies the reflection of your forthcoming light. That reflection is the living life force of the unconscious/higher mind; it is automatically balancing your intellect. As a result, when you speak your thoughts, you are right in the middle of your own conversation. It is so simple for you to create your own reality, so just stop your chattering, which is only you giving yourself more time to create your excuses. For goodness sake, give in to yourself!

The matter of physics, or the Metaphysical language, is all about earning your own responsibility to release each one of your thoughts; it is about exercising your inner and outer levels as one. Let them echo through one another. Let the illusion begin! Look inside yourself, be still, and pause. By returning back to yourself, you are capable of surrendering to yourself, where your inner light allows you to see through the layers of your darkness. Nothing stays the same, as time does not allow it. Time is created through both time and space understanding, releasing, accepting, and then acting. Exactly the same as to how the human body and every other species that has evolved.

Through space, we arc our responsibility back to our self! This keeps us gravitized. Time also has its own mathematical equation as to how you measure yourself to find the space that your freedom is creating on your own behalf. The Laws of Attraction measure every thought that you think, also please remember, if you don't have the courage to release your past, you must see this outrageous thought through, again and again. Read Einstein's Theories of Relativity, in which he explains so beautifully exactly what I am explaining to you right now.

When I speak to you from the unconscious/higher mind, we find that the left brain controls the left side of the body, and the right brain controls the right. Everything that happens on the right side reflects on an inner level, that is why we shake hands with our right hand. Everything that happens on the left side reflects on an outer level. The left brain also reflects from the toes to the navel, and this is the area where we learn to "understand our self". It is the darkness, and it is where our fear has been instilled through the genes of our previous generations.

That fear is the primordial understanding. That is what we call the first dimension of the God, referred to through the stories of the Metaphysical myths as "EL", which means "Everlasting Life". As that darkness views itself, it automatically reaches up to create an acceptance of self through achieving a balance. That balance then harmonizes, and it is in this state of grace that we are free to create our own acceptance. This is known as the second dimension of the God, referred to in the Metaphysical agenda as the God "AN", which, when decoded through the Sacred Alphabet, means "Ascending through Nourishing". This area houses the inner library, where we store our information called the Soul Energy! It is our educational system, where we learn to accept and educate our self!

The Soul then begins to open itself up, freeing itself from the fear that we have placed around it. Remember that, when we can learn to accept our own thinking, it is the first step in the process of silencing the mind. We are bowing to our own inheritance, which creates a feeling of regeneration. That positive energy must continue on upwards into the upper half of the body. This action is created when we have found the freedom to act out our own responses.

The body starts to push itself upright, yearning for its next step, which magnifies time. It is where the action and the understanding come together, and it is also the formation of the unconscious/higher mind releasing itself through the world of the Divine. We have now brought together the third dimension of the God within, and, again through the mythical agenda, we refer to it as the Metaphysical God "EA", which means "Energizing the Ascension".

When we greet a friend in my country, we say, "G'day mate! How are you going?" This ancient word (g'day) is Aboriginal, also it comes from the Aramaic language of the God "Gudea". When we bring this word into the English language, we pronounce it as the God "EA", so, as we greet one another, we are calling and respecting one another as a God— the Godness within each of us. Nicely said, don't you think?

CHAPTER TWENTY FOUR

Time Is Not At All What It Seems

Time is as long as it takes you to understand the thought in your mind in your moment. That thought is symbolically construed to live one lifetime. Time is only here for the ego to expiate. Time is collecting information to be used in the future. Time is the black hole in the Universe, which portends the results of our thinking and reverses those thoughts back to us. We must understand ourselves before we can act, and we cannot act until we understand. That is one of the Laws of the Universe!

In ordinary states of awareness, time appears to flow linearly, with events occurring one after the other. So, does time flow? Well, you will probably find strange the fact that there is no evidence for it. Actually, if you go back to the concept of absolute space-time and special theory of relativity, you will even find that time does not have any flow at all. But how is that possible? Our notion of time on a daily basis clearly indicates time does pass. We clearly can say at this present moment I'm reading these very lines and few moments later this will be history (so future is where now becomes past).

Yes, time does pass, but for whom, each single entity creates their own time, which is not relevant to others. Their time evolves in another way (we are our own Universe). I found this very hard to believe in the beginning when my teacher Sharon Hotz, informed me that time was only on my side. It had nothing to do with her; therefore she could not interfere with my time. She could correct my explanation and invite me up another layer for me to see how I had spoken my words to her, this helped greatly. The only reason we require time in a third dimensional reality is for the sake of our ego. It needs to feel quantified before it goes on.

Myself personally, time means absolutely nothing to me. Why? I have mathematically evolved beyond it, therefore there is no need for me to require or request time. My Higher Self directs me to be in the right place at the right time. It is a quantum approach that I have earned where my higher self and I come together. When I am asked a question about a particular situation, in my "viewing" for the answer, all events exist simultaneously; I am viewing many scenarios at the same time (similar to a wall of computer monitors).

Everything has a reason to be involved in our three-dimensional time; everything has its own energy, even down to the minerals that create the head of a match or the cow in the paddock or the blade of grass it eats! Every single thing on this planet is quantified through the mathematics to be here, it has its own purpose for being here, and it fits with the Mosaic of life! If there was no need, it would not be in our presence. Even down to the smallest of bacteria. If it is present, there is a reason for it to be involved in our three-dimensional time.

This tick-tock of the quantum Universe must always keep rolling forward; as we roll forward, the past is travelling with us. Why? It has nowhere to go! Please remember we are advancing our past as we advance our own future. In addition, as it is stated: "Stop the clock and you stop motion", not time. Again, may I remind you that time is only for the ego, the ego is our driving force, when we hesitate through not being sure of ourselves, our excuse is time is not on our side. Yes it is, but only until we have quantified the thought in our mind, in this moment. Once quantified, we are free to move on.

A short mention regarding our brain; this wonderful internal machine relates only to the unconscious/higher mind. Therefore, it works beyond time, if you are in a positive motion there is no need for hesitation, your brain automatically has your next thought waiting for you. Just know that you know, that you know, that you know! The more you get to know, the less time you need. If your future action is on a roll forward, you do not require time. Things will automatically happen on your behalf, for you. You are your inner and your outer—your higher self, all at the same time. This is what we term enlightenment!

If your thoughts are positive through believing in self, your heart beats to a different tune. Your heartbeat rectifies the brain, which reorganises the brain with confidence to ascertain that you are there in communion with it. Why should it hesitate? We do that by ourselves, and the only reason we do so, is through us not having enough belief in self. Hoping this information helps a little more as I bring the onus back to you. If you require time, become aware of the excuses you're about to make!

Your next dimension of time is waiting in the wings to step forward and initiate you into your next earned wisdom; all of which collects through your own individual state of consciousness opening you up into the next lesson of statehood, which is the banner earned. Remember, the mathematics of quantum consciousness is the energy in motion. While the mathematics of the natural law is in a forward motion, time becomes irrelevant.

In a state of infinite existence where you occupy all space, there can be no experience of the passing of time.

Your Notes:

CHAPTER TWENTY FIVE

The Last Chapter

As stated previously you are your own Individual Universal Law; and, as you think, so, too, you create. You are given this gift to be in charge of how your thoughts create your world. As you allow one thought to finish itself, the next one is waiting to release itself to you. Your next thought will wait patiently until you are silent enough to allow it to come through. It doesn't matter how high or how far out there you go, another challenge will always be ahead of you. Your challenges never cease; the completion of one challenge, allows the next one to step forward towards you. The difference is that the more you walk inside yourself, the smaller those challenges will become. As you grow through your own self-confidence, you will feel yourself becoming taller, as you release your inner light back out to the whole of humanity. Yes, you have already read this before, I am just reminding you of you. You are not on the same level you were, before you picked up this book to read.

Your life is a miracle; it is the co-creation of you. Be peaceful with yourself, and all will be revealed. Know that you know everything; you don't have to understand it straight away; just know that you know it. Research every cell of your body, and you will understand that each cell is a reflection giving its life force over to you.

And also remember that, as it is within, so, too, it is out there; every other human on this planet is representing to you a part of yourself. Always remember we are all one.

Once you understand what your Individual Universal Law is, keep yourself focused, and you will be able to fulfil all your desires. Life will bring you up, through the temperance of your Soul, and, when you can define this inner education, you will become an aspect of the Divine Light.

The Laws of the Universe are involved with you closely as you evolve up to the next step. These Laws do not come down to meet you. They invite you up to enter up into their light where you receive the contentment which is called enlightenment to release your peace within. The word "LOVE" springs to attention here in my writings, as it is this word that corroborates with the planetary species as they harmonically dance in unison with one another. The heart must be opened for this feeling to swirl in a clockwise direction to generate itself out to the outer boundaries of this wonderful place we call home. Being enlightened is when the Universe works for you; it is not you working for the Universe, so, through trusting the self, you become your own Master, and you guide your own light.

These teachings are not to tell you what to do; they are to place you in a situation that, in this moment, is beyond yourself. These teachings are to get you to step outside yourself in order to see who you are without the support of your fear.

Take us the foxes
The little foxes,
That spoil our vines
For our vines, have tender grapes.

Dare to be a Daniel,
Dare to stand alone,
Dare to have a purpose true, and
Dare to make it known.

Those two sayings, were my brother's favourite mottos as a child, he repeated them all his short life. The first one is relative to the little negative thoughts that you keep on excusing yourself with, which interrupt your flow. "For our vines have tender grapes", is for you to progress onwards and upwards, your vine or thoughts must keep advancing forward. The second one speaks for itself. It does not mean that you have to live alone; they mean that, in your mind's eye, you can hold your own focus—your own light—and still be aware of everything that is happening around you, as well as on this planet. Stand alone and release the sound of your voice out there. You are your own best teacher, and the more you centre your mind, the more the Laws of the Universe will reward you. This journey of enlightenment is yours and yours alone, so make your light bright.

You, as a member of humanity, have evolved through your family lineage to live on this planet, to create a service to self, and, in return, to share your earnings with mankind. You have a journey to equate and balance the past generations of your family in order for you to think clearly within yourself. All of this creates an inner freedom for the next generation to inherit. It is the same story for every human who has ever been, is, or will become. Revelations 1:8 reminds us that, "I am the Alpha and Omega, the beginning and the ending, saith the Lord, which is, and which was, and which is to come, the Almighty."

The journey of humanity states thus; we must come up through the primordial evolution of self—which means accepting all of the species that have evolved before us, as they are the make-up of our conscious thinking—before we can enter into the discovery of life and what it holds for us. We are here to learn the truth of self, and this creates the opening and unfolding of the Soul of self, which, in turn creates the life force of the spirit of God within self. It is that spirit of self that connects us into the Collective Consciousness. The Collective Consciousness climbs through the evolution of building itself, layer by layer or step by step, through mathematically aligning.

As we birth through and unfold our emotional intelligence, it sets the scene for the next phase of our life, helping us to adjust and opening us up into the hierarchical mind that we so often ignore through the lack of trust and belief in what we can become. We look for the easy way out. We tend to want to pass on our responsibilities to others, in order to free us of the temptation of standing out in front of our own illusion— the illusion that has the possibility of becoming our reflection, where we become free to release the light of our Soul. Once that primordial mind has balanced, we strive to adhere to the belief that we have attained through reminding ourselves of what we have become.

The photographic memory that is autonomically registered in every cell in our body holds all the records of evolution and conciliation. This is our Individual Universal Law, our inner universe, and they reflect back to us the Laws of the Universe. They hold and support us through every moment of time that we have endured as a species. All of which gives our intelligence the opportunity to advance us into becoming a greater species, where we learn to abide by the truth that we have strived for.

Once we begin to accept this inner wisdom as our own responsibility, we learn to educate our fear; it, in turn, learns to unfold itself and traverse up into our higher intelligence, which opens up the restrictions that we have placed upon ourselves. The creation of self then combines and heralds our forthcoming earnings. These earnings are then inherited by and with the Collective Consciousness of all, which is where God, (Greatest Oracle of the Divine) as we know it, redesigns and advances our program, which escalates in and through our self-worth. We release the pleasure of not only achieving, but also of returning to those less fortunate than ourselves. It is called tithing, and that tithing is rewarded to the planet as a whole. We are allowing the future to release on our behalf, which means acting out through the Oracle of our life, not to our detriment.

When we understand the depths of these Laws of the Universe, we begin to realize the potentiality of the unconscious/higher mind. Every thought we think and everything we do is added up and measured and they are registered throughout the Laws of the Universe and mirrored through the light of our Collective Consciousness, which we now know holds the keys to our intelligence. That reflection is then passed back to us as our payment from God.

I bow to each of you who understand these words in your truth. I salute you on the rest of your life's journey, and may you inherit the wind. The wind still plays an important role in every moment of my life. Our training in Shamanism is to become the Breath of God—the Atum, Atem, Atom, and Adam. Those principles are self-regenerating the cells of the planet, which holds and supports our breath. I must end this book as I began it, and bring this circle to its completion. May you learn, through the unfolding of your Individual Universal

Law, to dance along with the Collective Consciousness that is the Law(s) of the Universe. Those Collective Laws are freely available to us all. In that way, we receive the possibility of inheriting the wind, which is the Breath of the God.

The next instalment of your life is beginning in "Book II: Decoding Thought", and my aim is to introduce you to the power of your inner energy, so that you will understand how it can balance and become your eternal energy. Thank you for reading my written words in this part of my story.

Blessed Be, Omni

Appendix A. Glossary

Aura: Energy of our soul, surrounding every individual human being; it is our life force.

Balancing the mind: Through conscious awareness of your internal dialogue. Is the self-talk positive? If not, stop the chattering mind (repose the ego). Breathe and prepare the mind by sitting in silence (similar to a reset on a computer). Then focus and use words to honour yourself, allowing the correct thought to come through (use positive affirmations). Be the personality of Self Esteem—Regal—be in your Royalness. Always remember the self, you are the most important person on this Earth.

Believe in yourself: As you begin to believe in yourself, your Soul gives you never-ending gifts of knowledge. To believe in yourself takes a tremendous amount of courage, and that courage will lead you into other parallel worlds of existence. Those worlds align within and open you up to your inner worlds, where you can thank yourself for having earned the freedom to use them to promote your tomorrows.

Empowering ourselves: When your belief in self builds upon its own strength and creates your next positive thought, your life becomes so much easier for you to manage. Are you changing the molecular structure of your whole body by thinking a positive thought in regard to yourself?

English Language: We refer to the English language as the language of the angels, which brings us closer into the connection of telepathic communication. The English language is the last language to this third-dimensional planet, and it has now become the business language for the whole of humanity. It is from here that we can absorb ourselves up into the fourth dimension.

Hierarchical mind: Also known as the Higher Self

Individual Universal Law: We are each our own Universe with our own Individual Universal Law, and we exist within a greater Universe that has its own proprietary law as well. You are your own Individual Universal Law; and, as you think, so, too, you create. You are given this gift to be in charge of how your thoughts create your world. As you allow one thought to finish itself, the next one is waiting to release itself to you. Your next thought will wait patiently until you are silent enough to allow it to come through. Your Individual Universal Law is not created by what you do, but, rather, by your silent thoughts, regressions (thinking in the past), joys, frustrations, and peace. It is the energy and evolution of your emotional intelligence and how you connect to you.

Intellectual Light: It is the intellectual light from your thinking that is your creation, not necessarily what you do, but rather, how you think to do things. (The higher mind is the intellectual light. Through the inner strength that we confidently release through our right brain, it releases the memories that have been genetically implanted into the aura of our cells; from there, it connects through to the inner vision, which becomes the intellectual light of information that the left brain receives. As each human evolves into his/her own emotional heritage (DNA), through concentrating on his/her own self-worth, the transformation of each related word mirrors and reflects through that person's intellectual light, and this then returns into his/her thoughts). This intellectual light is the compulsive positive energy or irresistible urge that surges through our life force.

Karma: Karma, or the "Kha-Rha-Mha", if we explain it correctly, for this goes back to the early language of the Armenians and the hieroglyphs of Egypt. If we pronounce it in its correctness, it is the cause and effect, or the accidental and occidental.

Accident: Our accidents are what we have produced for ourselves through our thinking. Our thinking produces an energy. For example, anger can build up in negative energy and if not released through reasoning an accident will occur.

Occidental: The occidental is the explanation, as to how we have gathered and achieved the accident in the first place. The occident is how we created that accident through our mathematics being realigned to our thinking. The occident is another way to explain the Laws of the Universe in action. The mathematical codes have clicked into action and been brought together!

Laws of the Universe: It is our Individual Universal Law creating the Laws of the Universe! It is where we all become involved, and, through time and cause and effect, we have created and advanced our evolution for all humanity to inherit. These Laws of the Universe are also known as the following: Collective Consciousness, Collective Library of the Consciousness, World Consciousness, Collective Inheritance, Collective Memory, Collective Mind, Collective Soul of the God Force, Akashic Hall of Records, Hall of Recognition, Soul Energy of Collective Consciousness and have many other terminologies. The Laws of the Universe (Collective Consciousness) registers all our conscious thinking, which must return to the conscious mind in order for our energy to continue to grow through the human evolution. The past is still alive in the Collective Consciousness; that Collective Inheritance is all of our thinking and evolution. We cannot forget yesterday, but we can absorb it; we can soak it up into our own consciousness and use it in the moment.

Ley Lines: We have electromagnetic energy ley lines that connect with our internal meridian lines to assist with our human potentiality. Throughout your life's journey, twelve ley lines will unfold from inside the base of your brain (which begins at the base of the spine), and research explains this as your central nervous system intellectually unfolding itself. This energy is called the "Chi", through the Asian Principles, where it becomes a vortex that you are creating through your positive behaviour and your thoughts begin to collect, where they create a spiral, which continues up into the pyramidal section in the base of the skull. Through this spiral collecting its own life force, it is swept up into the medulla oblongata section of the brain, which symbolically represents the crossroads.

Life Program: Your life program was created through your parents' DNA, which provided the basic principles for you to become you. Your task is to unfold yourself through the disadvantages of your parents' judgment and (mis) understanding themselves! You have chosen to live what your parents were too afraid to face through their acceptance of self as they understood it, and, more importantly, you have also chosen to live their gains. Your life program keeps on creating itself through each of your thoughts building upon the other, and the transformation continues until you have taken your last breath. That energy force field grows in strength and opens you up into your Higher—or heavenly— Self. That Higher Self follows you through every thought you think, always encouraging you to create and expand your thinking.

Meridians The meridians, respond to the energy of the unconscious/higher mind relating to the responses created throughout our nervous systems. You cannot see these meridians with the naked eye. They are the autonomic responses of language that flow up through your body from your toes, throughout the trunk and connecting through the heart, where they then flow down through your arms and reconnect back up to the yoke, or collarbone, where we carry and "shoulder" our responsibilities, and then entering up into the temple area of self.

Mythology: MY-THEOLOGY, my religion, my way of life. It is a coded intelligence that is implanted and stored in your force fields—now referred to as your aura, or the energy of your Soul.

Personalities of Self: Aspects of self. An emotion is a personality of yours or an aspect of self. Your responsibility lies with the relationship of self, through the power of beginning with just one positive thought.

Quest for the Metaphysical Pathway: Metaphysics is the mathematical measuring of the inner balance of the mind, which we call the "Phi" or "Pi". The Quest is one of learning first to silence and then to listen to our conscious and subconscious minds; this journey can take a while and once understood, we have the opportunity to always move forward and upwards to relying more on the totality of our unconscious/higher mind. (Soul/Higher Self).

Relationship of self: The blueprint from which your life manifests. The relationship of self is the way you relate to you. It is created by the thoughts you have about yourself, belief in self, the emotions you feel about yourself, your judgements about yourself, your perception your self-worthiness and how you honour yourself—your internal dialogue to self. When your belief in self builds upon its own strength and creates your next positive thought, your life becomes so much easier for you to manage.

Releasing negative thought, experience or fear: If that same memorial negative thought, experience or fear, is created back into your thinking again, you must stop it before it becomes greater. I still remember my traffic lessons when I went to school: **stop**, **look**, and **listen**. Try to search beyond the moment to see how this energy or thought re-created itself. It is not a learning experience; this time, it becomes an earning. There is a big difference between learning and earning: the former means "looking at", and the later means "looking through". Our Higher Self—our unconscious/higher mind—presents all of these experiences for us. It gives us the opportunity for our thoughts to repeat throughout our life, until we can find the strength to overcome them. One thing in life is certain: You cannot run away from yourself. There is nowhere to hide! You create your fear in the moment through your thinking. Write this affirmation down: "My fear is created by me, as I am refusing to live and accept this Divine moment in my life."

Sacred Alphabet: When we go back to the first language of man, we can see the evolution of the Sacred Alphabet, as well as how the collection of our tribal heritage has programmed our own language into us, which autonomically creates our own intelligence.

Sacred Numerology: Metaphysical Numerology works through the interpretation of the etheric levels. Each number is created through a resonance.

Sonic sound: When we raise the level of our thinking and therefore vibration, this is when we harmonize our thoughts with the potential of "the all" the unseen, where the level of our thought creates and manifests into physical reality, matching the experience.

Soul Energy of Collective Consciousness (Laws of the Universe): A mathematical program of all that is. The mathematics of the Universe, which can be equated to pure energy, has always been here long before our gestation into human. This Universe and the millions of other Universes have always been in existence as a mathematical equation. In totality, it became the Divine Intervention or what we term as Natural Law; which we now refer to as the Collective Consciousness—The Laws of the Universe.

Structure of our brain/mind: Our brain has two sides, left and right. Left brain is our logic (conscious mind). The left brain is our masculine side; our ego, our primal fear, and as stated our logic. It represents how we are representing ourselves to others through releasing from within. Our left brain, our conscious self, is responsible for the first and second-dimensional mind. The right brain is our emotions (subconscious mind). The right brain is our feminine side, our inner creativity. We give out to others with the right side, and our energy in motion—or emotion—creates itself from how we are giving and receiving to and from the self. The right brain represents what we are doing to ourselves within, and what we are capable of receiving through ourselves–through our being aware of that giving. Our right brain, our subconscious self; it is responsible for the third dimension and the relationship to the introduction of the fourth dimension.

The balance of both brains is the doorway up into our unconscious/higher mind. The unconscious/higher mind (Soul/Higher Self) is the freedom with which we can tune into ourselves, but only when the other two have balanced through our attitude to our self. We touch and connect to our unconscious/higher mind, as the other two brains encompass the Soul through looking into one another.

Universal Language of Babylon: The language of the planet became the language of Babylon—to understand the language of the earth. "Bja-ab-EL-on" through the Sacred Alphabet. ("Bja", of man through the explanations of the Egyptian hieroglyphs. The iron represents the core of our being, our bone structure; our DNA is a creation whose composition is identical to the planet that we inhabit. "EL": metaphysically interpreted as the first of the ancient Gods—Everlasting Life—Everlasting Life is the Oracle nourishing us through the Divine Oracle nurturing the self. The Oracle as you speak your words through harmonizing your mind, you release your own Oracle.

Weather patterns, dis-eases, viruses, and wars: are all creations of the atmospheric conditions of the Collective Consciousness; they are the results of the thinking of this planet. The energy collects itself through the mathematics of the Laws of the Universe.

Your Notes:

Books By O.M. Kelly (Omni)

Decoding The Mind Of God
Author O.M. Kelly's seminal work, "Decoding the Mind of God", is a compilation of nine volumes of metaphysical information based on the research into the coded information of the Laws of the Universe, also known as the Collective Consciousness, and represents a groundbreaking contribution to our understanding of the metaphysical universe. Now, all nine volumes are being released as separate, revised books, each offering a unique perspective on the universe's workings. Omni's work has been widely acclaimed for its depth of insight, and her contributions to the field of metaphysics have been groundbreaking.

The nine separate volumes encompassing:

The Laws of the Universe
Thought
Dis-Ease
Death
Sexuality and Spirituality
The Dolphin's Breath
Sacred Alphabet and Numerology
Sacred Fung Shwa
Extra-Terrestrial Intelligence.
Updated version of each book now being released separately.

Book I. Decoding The Laws Of The Universe
If you're looking to unlock the hidden potential within you and transform your life, "Decoding the Laws of the Universe" is the book for you. This powerful and insightful book is designed to help you understand the deeper, metaphysical aspects of life and tap into the transformative power of the universe utilising the secrets of our Individual Universal Law.

This book serves to introduce you into the secrets of our Individual Universal Law. This amazing knowledge and wisdom, is transformative on a personal level and creates the opportunity for you to interrelate with the Laws of the Universe. Throughout this book, you will dive deep into the inner workings of your mind and discover the hidden laws that govern your life. You will learn about the alchemy of the mind and how to harness its power to create positive change in your life and the world around you. Through the lens of Metaphysical philosophy, you will gain a new perspective on the world and your place in it. You will learn how the universe communicates with you through coded intelligence and how to unlock the hidden messages that are all around you.

This book is a journey for personal transformation and spiritual growth. Take a voyage of exploration of the expansive vistas of information discovering the codes of Metaphysics and the Quest of Life. You will learn the Metaphysical coded wisdom of the ancients for the necessary mind elements to transit into a higher mindset. Explore the secret relationship between the Earth and human beings, the higher mind, the Metaphysical journey, the importance of self, belief in self, the codes of mythology, a higher level of attainment, releasing the past, fears and evolving one's light on a Metaphysical level, what causes stress, work place promotion and why it does not happen, and many other topics. Included is a short overview of the conventional Twelve Laws of the Universe.

Book II. Decoding Thought
Welcome to a journey of self-discovery and exploration of the mysteries of the universe. "Decoding Thought" is a ground-breaking book that explores the power of the mind and the principles of metaphysical thought. Through a deep exploration of the mind and body connection, the author provides readers with insights to unlock the full potential of their thoughts. This book provides a guide to harnessing the power of the mind to create the life you desire. With explanations of metaphysical principles, the book makes these often complex concepts accessible to readers. "Decoding Thought" takes you on a journey through the vast landscape of the human mind. Explore the mysteries of thought power, and how it can shape our reality and transform our lives. The power of thought is not just a theoretical concept. It is a tangible force that can be harnessed to bring about significant changes in our lives.

This book can expand your consciousness and open your mind to new possibilities. By exploring the metaphysical principles that underlie our existence, you can gain a new perspective on life and the world around you. This book provides through a metaphysical interpretation explanations into the various aspects of thought power, including how it is linked to our DNA, and the roles played by the pituitary and pineal glands in our thought processes. O.M. Kelly also explains the metaphysical language in reference to the codes of the Egyptian Philosophies, the Bible, myths, cultures, and how they connect to the power of thought. The journey continues with a deep dive into the inner Secret School of Metaphysics, where we discover the Alchemy of the Brain and the pathway to our truth. Discover the unconscious/higher mind, and our Life Quest, which opens the doors to the Psychometric Consciousness. Through the lens of metaphysical interpretation, you will gain a new perspective on the impact of thought on our mental and emotional states that includes a look at Depression, Coping with Change and how to retrain our brain patterns to be positive and moving forward for our Financial Abundance and manifesting prosperity. The book ends with a brief overview of the brain/mind, and a short Q&A on thought power. This metaphysical book on the power of thought is a guide to discovering your true potential and creating the life you desire.

"Decoding Thought" is a must-read for anyone seeking to unlock the full potential of their mind and harness the power of the universe to create a life of fulfilment and this book serves as an invaluable resource.

Book III. Decoding Dis-Ease

Introducing "Decoding Dis-Ease" a Metaphysical Interpretation into understanding the intricate web of factors that contribute to our health and well-being. From the author of several groundbreaking works on the interaction of the mind and body, this book delves into a wide range of topics related to dis-ease. It is a fascinating and insightful book that offers a fresh perspective on health and healing. It is a must-read for anyone interested in the mind-body connection.

Readers will be inspired to embark on a quest of discovering the codes within themselves, recognizing that every cell in our body is pure Cosmic Consciousness. They will also gain a deeper understanding of specific health topics such as the thyroid, the kidneys, men's problems, and many other topics from a Metaphysical perspective. The book also examines how a dis-ease is given to us in group energy and the complex interplay between our bodies and minds, and how every human has the consequences of all that we do and experience.

Book IV. Decoding Death

Looking for a thought-provoking exploration of death and the afterlife? Look no further than O.M. Kelly's book, "Decoding Death".

"Decoding Death takes us on a transformative Metaphysical journey through the mysteries of the Universe. O.M. Kelly—known as Omni—provides an expanded horizon of possibilities, awareness, and a transformative perspective. In this book, Omni delves into a wide range of topics related to dying and death, from the loss of a loved one to a viewing of the afterlife. Omni has a unique ability to view the Laws of the Universe using her extraordinary state of heightened awareness and multi-dimensional perception and through the lens of metaphysics offers a unique perspective on the nature of death and what it means for the human experience.

Omni shares personal experiences and stories, including the passing of her late husband, brother, and parents, and offers a metaphysical insight for those dealing with loss and grief. She explores the transformational process of death and the potential for spiritual growth and enlightenment. The book explains that the human experience of death is part of a larger Universal process that is ultimately guided by a higher intelligence referred to as God (Laws of the Universe/Collective Consciousness) or whatever name you prefer. Omni's exploration of death is both metaphysically comprehensive and thought-provoking, offering readers a deep and nuanced understanding of one of life's greatest mysteries. With chapters on the Three Doorways—Three Stages of Death, The Quantum Hologram—Why a partner dies for the other partner to progress in the "Journey of Life", The Passing to the Afterlife, and many other enlightening chapters, "Decoding Death" offers a unique viewpoint. By drawing on a range of religious, philosophical, and metaphysical perspectives, Omni offers a compelling vision of the human experience of death and its role in the larger Universal Law.

Book V. Decoding Sexuality And Spirituality

Welcome to "Decoding Sexuality and Spirituality" by O.M. Kelly. In this book, explore the fascinating relationship between our sexuality and spirituality, and how these two aspects of ourselves are intimately intertwined. Delve into the concept that sexuality is the doorway to our spirituality, and examine the powerful and transformative energy that is generated when we fully embrace our sexual selves. The book also explores the notion of the metaphysical orgasmic cloud, and how it can be used to deepen our connection to our spiritual selves. We will also examine the role of marriage in our sexual and spiritual lives.

For women, the book offers a unique perspective on the journey of embracing sexuality and spirituality, as well as insights into the different stages of life and how they impact our sexual and spiritual selves. Drawing on both ancient wisdom traditions and metaphysical mythology, the book examines the myth of Hercules and how it relates to our sexual intelligence. By decoding the symbolism of this myth, we can gain a deeper understanding of the ways in which our sexuality and spirituality intersect and influence each other. So if you are ready to embark on a journey of self-discovery and unlock the true potential of your sexual and spiritual selves, then "Decoding Sexuality and Spirituality" is the book for you.

VI. Decoding The Dolphin's Breath

"Decoding The Dolphin's Breath" by O.M. Kelly (Omni) is a captivating exploration of the relationship between humans and dolphins. The book begins with a poignant account of a real-life encounter between the author and a group of wild dolphins, setting the stage for a deep dive into the spiritual and metaphysical significance of dolphins. This captivating book takes readers on a journey into the heart of the dolphin-human relationship, exploring the ways in which these majestic creatures can help us attune to the power of free will, and telepathic communication.

Throughout the Laws of Shamanism the wonderful Dolphin in consciousness, represents the attainment we can reach through ourselves earning our freedom of will. This book explains the benefits of the dolphins breath—the why and how we use the breath that influences our divine mentality. Further, it's a story which reveals how the dolphins have taught us the process to be free of fear, and to tap into the Language of Babylon—to understand the language of Earth. One of the key themes of the book is the idea that dolphins are always breathing their total freedom of thought, and the author provides insights into how humans can learn from this remarkable trait. The book also invites readers to embark on a journey into understanding the telepathic communication of whales and dolphins. Inclusive in the book is a written meditation which assists you to connect to the external consciousness and release the fear that you have wrapped around yourself for protection.

Overall, this book offers a unique and fascinating perspective on the metaphysics of dolphins, and will appeal to anyone interested in spirituality, and the power of the mind.

Book VII. Decoding The Sacred Alphabet And Numerology

This book offers a myriad of explanations concerning the higher consciousness in relationship to names, places and numbers. "Decoding The Sacred Alphabet & Numerology" by O.M. Kelly (Omni) is a thought-provoking and enlightening read that

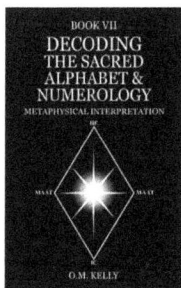

offers a unique perspective on the metaphysical world of letters and numbers.

Omni's insights and teachings are sure to inspire readers to deepen their understanding of the ancient sacred codes to names of places, your name and the sacred alphabet. The author also delves into the practice of metaphysical numerology, which involves using numerical values to interpret personality traits, life paths, and other aspects of a person's life. Omni explains how metaphysical numerology can be used to gain insight into our spiritual path and to better understand our purpose in life. Your ability to decipher the Sacred Alphabet and Numerology codes commonly and constantly presented to you throughout your life, will open opportunities to expand your consciousness and awareness you never thought possible.

Embark on a journey through the myth of Babylon and Shambhala and discover the sacred language that connects us all. Explore Luxor, the Delta Giza Saqqara and Faiyum, and Solomon's Temple, and uncover the mysteries of Akhenaton and Tomb KV-63. Find out how to unravel the threads of your DNA and unlock the ancient knowledge of the Old Aramaic Story of Aladdin and the Lamp. Explore Grecian stories through the Metaphysical language and travel along the Old Silk Road. Discover the Shamanic inheritance of numbers and their meanings, and learn how we rely on numbers to read the hidden language of the universe. Join O.M. Kelly on a journey of self-discovery and uncover the divine language within.

Book VIII. Decoding Sacred Fung Shwa
Introducing "Decoding Sacred Fung Shwa", the revolutionary guide to understanding and harnessing the energy within your home and yourself. In this book, author O.M. Kelly (Omni), has introduced a metaphysical sixth element that takes our understanding of energy to the next level. By incorporating "Your Life Force," we gain deeper insight into the connection between our homes and our emotional well-being. Discover the power of Fung Shwa and learn how to use it to create a balanced and harmonized environment that supports your mind, body, and Soul.

The book explains the meaning of Sacred Fung Shwa to the Shamanistic principles that underpin it. Delve into the metaphysical medicine wheel and explore the elements of life, before moving on to practical applications of Fung Shwa in the home.

Learn how to visualize your home as a collective energy and clear the clutter to enhance its flow. Discover your Astrological colours and how they can be used in Fung Shwa design, from the kitchen to the bedroom and beyond. Explore the compatibility of personal colours in relationships, and discover the power of paintings, pictures, and mirrors to enhance your home's energy.

But Fung Shwa isn't just about the home—we also explore its applications in the office environment and in small retail businesses. Learn how to apply Fung Shwa principles to a clothing store, shoe store, or café, even discover the role of Fung Shwa in money, and to Metaphysical Numerology.

Throughout it all, we focus on the quest of life and how Fung Shwa can help you achieve your goals and live your best life. So what are you waiting for? Dive into the world of Fung Shwa and transform your home, your business, and your life today!

Book IX. Decoding Extra-Terrestrial Intelligence

Are you ready to embark on a journey of self-discovery? Look no further than O.M. Kelly's groundbreaking book, Book IX "Decoding Extra-Terrestrial Intelligence". Through metaphysical interpretation, O.M. Kelly (Omni) has unlocked the secrets of the universe and revealed that the key to our next step in human evolution lies within ourselves. This book will show you how to tap into the indelible imprint of holographic importance that is seeded within every human, and unleash the Extra-Terrestrial Intelligence that resides within you. Omni shares her own personal journey of encountering Beings of Light and how it has transformed her understanding of the universe and humanity's place within it.

Omni presents the concept that we all have Extra-Terrestrial Intelligence, and have the ability to tap into the vast knowledge and secrets of the universe. The ancient civilizations left behind clues and teachings about this metaphysical existence and it is up to us to continue to uncover and advance the way we think. Through this journey of life, we can unlock the secrets of our own consciousness and tap into the full potential of our existence. This is a fascinating exploration of the mysteries of the universe and the potential for our own personal evolution.

Readers who are interested in self-transformation through universal truths, Metaphysical exploration for personal growth and a journey of self-discovery would be interested in reading this insightful book on contact with Beings of Light and Extra-terrestrial Intelligence, exploring ancient civilizations and the knowledge they possessed about the universe and the human mind.

Power Thought for the Day Oracle Book

"Power Thought For The Day Oracle Book" provides insights to assist you on your life path. Through the "Totem" energy of all, the ancient species that have evolved before us, represent an emotional inheritance that we can rely on to sustain the moment. Each species that has evolved on this planet is recorded into our cellular memory. This book with 22 Major Arcana Shamanic Power Animal Totems provides a contemporary metaphysical interpretation symbolic of our evolution. By selecting a page of the book the Shamanic animal will provide an insight in how you are thinking at this moment in time. Through the contemporary Laws of Shamanism (with a metaphysical interpretation), O.M. Kelly (Omni) has produced a book that will assist the "Path of the Initiate" in emotional intelligence when our mind is in the field of doubt. When we become aware of how we are thinking it is a catalyst for transformation. This compact little book is a handy 4 x 7 inches or 10.2 x 17.8 cm to fit into your pocket or handbag.

How to use the book:
Our higher mind has no time; it steps into and works on behalf of the thought of the moment. This book encompasses 22 Major Totem Power representations, symbolic of our evolution. Close your eyes and inhale and exhale a deep breath and relax and allow yourself no thought as you select the right page of the Shamanic animal presented in this book. The right page will always appear for you at the right moment and you will discover how the power animals are working with you for insight into their wisdom. Different power animals come into our lives at various phases offering messages to guide us on our path.

Decoding the Shaman Within

In "Decoding the Shaman Within" international author O.M. Kelly (Omni) shares her Shamanic metaphysical journey. It would be termed a contemporary Shamanic initiation journey; a powerful spiritual enlightenment and transformational voyage of discovering the codes of Metaphysics and the Quest of Life. Through the sacred passage of time Omni discovered the secret codes of the Collective Consciousness (Laws of the Universe) to trek a higher level of consciousness. Throughout

Omni's training to receive the breath of Shamanism, many Elders from other cultures came to Australia and initiated her into their own tribal laws. Most of these Elders were men who arrived on Omni's doorstep uninvited but had received the call from the Universe to pass on their knowledge. Those magnificent people who had also earned their Shamanic experiences, only stayed long enough to give Omni their gift of consciousness and to initiate her into a new Shamanic name, which their tribe had bestowed, and then they disappeared out of Omni's life as quickly as they had come into it.

The Shamanic path in a Metaphysical perspective is the oldest pathway of the tribal law through the evolution of humanity. The Shaman is trained in the ancient language that is instilled in every genetic code that humanity carries within their DNA; you either have the opportunity to open it up and use it, or you just don't bother and choose to ignore it! It is as simple as that!

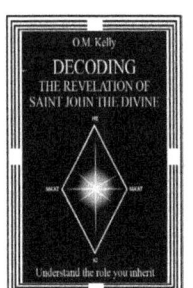

Decoding the Revelation of Saint John the Divine: Understand the role you inherit

The amazing breakthrough book "Decoding the Revelation of Saint John the Divine: Understand the role you inherit", is for anyone with an open, inquiring mind, seeking answers to the surreal descriptions of Earth's final days.

Through years of research O.M. Kelly interprets the cryptology behind the codes of mythology and various religions and has Metaphysically interpreted how the Holy Bible had been written through the original codex of Egyptology. The biblical stories were collected and condensed through the educated minds of that time.

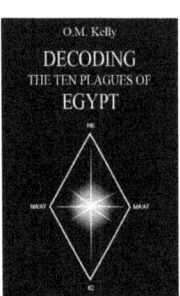

Decoding the Ten Plagues of Egypt

"Decoding the Ten Plagues of Egypt" presents a fresh insight into understanding the hidden structure of the language of how the Bible was written. The reader is introduced to the step by step Metaphysical decoding of the mystifying language, regarding the plagues from the Book of Exodus, Chapters: 7-12 in the Bible.

For the first time in contemporary history the essence of the Book of Exodus and its previously unsolved intriguing language will be revealed to provide deeper knowledge and clearer perception to unlock the significance the Book of Exodus is explaining to us.

Decoding Dreams

In "Decoding Dreams" international author O.M. Kelly (Omni), introduces a metaphysical interpretation of the dreams we dream. At times, we may believe that dreams allow us to peer into another world. O.M. Kelly provides the codes for us to understand that other world of dreams—or, through the Shamanic Principles, our "Vision Worlds". Dreams are created through your unconscious/higher mind communicating back to you; dreams are reminding you of the lessons that you need to understand regarding yourself. You cannot hear them if your mind is filled with incessant chatter. The ego refuses to conform when it is in control of the moment. Dreams can range from a pleasant dream, which could be a recommendation to add to what you are doing, to a nightmare, which is a wake-up call from your higher self regarding what you are doing to yourself. As you read this book, keep in mind that learning to metaphysically interpret your dreams is a step-by-step process. Areas covered in the book are: Dream Representations (Animal Kingdom and the Human Kingdom), Questions and Answers about Dreams, and Dream Interpretations.

Reprint coming in the near future.

www.ingramcontent.com/pod-product-compliance
Lightning Source LLC
Chambersburg PA
CBHW062036290426
44109CB00026B/2643